MASTER YOUR
DEBT

SLASH YOUR MONTHLY PAYMENTS
AND BECOME DEBT FREE

JORDAN E. GOODMAN
with BILL WESTROM

A Lynn Sonberg Book

WILEY

John Wiley & Sons, Inc.

Published by John Wiley & Sons, Inc., Hoboken, New Jersey.
Published simultaneously in Canada.

For general information on our other products and services or for technical support, please
contact our Customer Care Department within the United States at (800) 762-2974, outside the
United States at (317) 572-3993 or fax (317) 572-4002.

Wiley also publishes its books in a variety of electronic formats. Some content that appears in
print may not be available in electronic books. For more information about Wiley products,
visit our web site at www.wiley.com.

Library of Congress Cataloging-in-Publication Data:
Goodman, Jordan Elliot.
   Master your debt : slash your monthly payments and become debt free / Jordan E.
Goodman with Bill Westrom.
      p. cm.
   "A Lynn Sonberg book."
   Includes index.
   ISBN 978-0-470-48424-1 (cloth)
   1. Finance, Personal. 2. Debt. 3. Consumer credit. I. Westrom, Bill. II. Title.
   HG179.G6754 2010
   332.024'02—dc22

                                                                    2009041476

Printed in the United States of America

10 9 8 7 6 5 4 3 2 1

To my mother, Norma Bromberg Goodman, who first nurtured my interest in personal finance and who has always supported with love and enthusiasm everything I do.

Contents

Acknowledgments

M*aster Your Debt* would not have been possible without the generous and skillful contributions and extremely hard work of many talented people.

Foremost among these contributors is the team of Lynn Sonberg and Roger Cooper, who worked with me to hone the original idea of the book into its final form. Lynn skillfully guided the work from the original proposal through the research, writing, and editing process, always staying on top of the many details and maintaining a high standard for accuracy and clarity in the work. Roger was instrumental in framing the book's direction.

The writing and research team also did a remarkable job of combining skillful writing with exhaustive research on many topics related to debt and credit. Linda Stern used her many years of experience covering these topics at Reuters to write most of the text, weaving in many real-life case studies with all the explanations of the massive changes occurring almost daily in the debt and credit world. Bill Westrom of Truth in Equity (www.truthinequity.com), America's leading expert on mortgage and debt acceleration techniques, generously gave his knowledge, time, and resources to make sure that the sections on acceleration strategies that are so novel and powerful are as clearly and accurately explained as possible.

The team at John Wiley & Sons was also instrumental in making this project a reality. Executive Editor Debra Englander immediately embraced the concept of explaining how Americans need guidance in navigating the new and changing world of debt that is affecting them in their everyday lives. Kelly O'Connor edited the manuscript with great care and skill. Joan O'Neill, the publisher of the Professional and Trade Division at John Wiley, was extremely supportive of the book from conception through publication. Paul Dinovo created the eye-catching cover design. Senior Production Editor Stacey Fischkelta was responsible for overseeing the production of the book. The staff of Cape Cod Compositors, Inc., undertook the meticulous job of copyediting the manuscript. Herman Estevez skillfully took the photograph for the back cover.

My hope is that you, the reader of *Master Your Debt*, will use the knowledge you gain from this book to maximize the opportunities and avoid the pitfalls that this new era of debt brings to consumers in America. By combining the knowledge you glean from this book with all of the resources that I put at your disposal, you should be able to maintain the best credit rating possible, get the best deals available for all the kinds of loans you take on, and pay your debts off years sooner than you ever thought possible!

Jordan E. Goodman
January 1, 2010

INTRODUCTION

Master or Victim?
You Decide

Forget what you think you know about using other people's money. The game has completely changed.

The world of debt—everything from credit cards to mortgages and student loans—is completely different than it was just a few years ago, in the middle of the current decade. In this book I want to share the many secrets of debt management I've discovered that can help consumers all along the credit spectrum. I've studied the latest products and the newest rules, and also have some good information about the kinds of loans and credit card deals we can expect to see in the future. I want to share that with everyone, but mostly, I want everyone who reads this book to understand this: You can master debt and make it work for you. You can win the debt game.

The financial marketplace is always evolving, but recent developments have been especially dramatic—a sea change brought about by a credit crisis, a deep recession, and a new administration. Many loan products that were prevalent don't even exist now, and there are new ones taking their place. Those easy zero percent interest credit card deals have dried up, as have the most exotic mortgages and the "Bad credit? No problem!" attitudes of many car dealers. Private Student lenders have left the business in droves and may disappear altogether.

Now there is a different debt industry to take the place of the one that used to exist. There are new credit card rules, new student loan plans, and new mortgage modification programs. It's a whole new ball game.

So, yes—forget what you used to know. The financial market-place that we are dealing with going forward is not the one we had. Like every other wrenching economic shift, this change will produce new winners and new debt-destroyed victims.

More than ever before, the winners will be those people who are proactive about taking control of their financial destiny. Savvy consumers understand that the business of debt thrives on their remaining uneducated and passive. Those people who learn the new rules, find the new products, and make the right moves will become debt masters: They will be able to borrow money when they need it, pay it off cheaply and quickly, and sleep well at night.

That's why I wanted to write this book and put it in your hands as quickly as possible. I have spent my entire professional life offering specific, actionable, impartial advice to financial consumers, starting with my 18 years at *Money* magazine. I have learned whom to trust, whom *not* to trust, and how to tell the difference. This may be the first book you see that includes details of the new government mortgage and credit card programs, and I rushed to complete it so you could use it as you begin to master your debt in this new era.

In it are the strategies, resources, and techniques that will make you a debt master. It is replete with the latest rules and regulations out of Washington and the newest products from Wall Street and your neighborhood mortgage broker. It includes products and strategies that are so new, most people have never even heard of them. And it also includes the wisdom I've picked up in over 30 years of observing the marketplace and how it works.

I Hear What You Are Saying

I travel—a lot. As a financial journalist and educator, I speak to all sorts of groups; I appear on television, the radio, and on my own MoneyAnswers web site, and I get a steady stream of feedback from consumers who have questions about their finances.

And what I have been hearing is this: anger, worry, and confusion.

- In Cincinnati, I spoke to Julian, a homeowner who was trying to refinance his home. With good credit scores and a steady job, he wasn't expecting any problems. But in six months there were four foreclosures on his street, and Julian's home, which had been valued at $300,000 just six months earlier, was now appraised at $55,000. That's $245,000 in equity up in smoke—and forget about the refi.

- In Virginia, I spoke with Chris. He had put almost $100,000 of home repairs and renovations on credit cards charging him around 4 percent interest. He had been paying his bills automatically, online and on time, without reading them carefully. So he failed to notice that his card issuers yanked his borrowing power and raised his interest rates all the way up to 26 percent. Now he is struggling just to stay even.
- In New York, I talked to Phyllis and Greg. They seem to be living the American dream: They have their own graphic arts business and two great kids. But they have so much student debt they don't think they'll ever be able to buy a home. And they are flying without a health insurance safety net, living in fear of the medical emergency that will make their whole carefully calculated plan tumble down.

Those are just three stories among many, but they summarize the prevailing mood: People feel like they did everything they were supposed to; they played by the rules, and they have still gotten the short end of the financial stick. They are getting beaten up by factors over which they have no control, and they don't know what to do.

You Have Power

Bankers and other professionals like you to feel powerless. They love dealing with customers who are uneducated about the details of their business. They like to bully you into feeling too dumb or hopeless to ask questions.

That's nonsense. Financial consumers today have more power and more information at their fingertips than they ever have had in the history of American capitalism. Online brokers, online financial calculators, self-managed retirement accounts, and books like this all put the power in your hands to manage your own finances and wrest control from the banker bullies. They still compete for your dollar, and they can no longer count on winning it by keeping you in the dark about how the system works.

Use your power. Educate yourself about the new ways of the debt world, and your choices in it. Demand satisfaction and decent treatment from your lenders, and use the new products and re-sources at your disposal to put your debt and your cash to work for you. Read, study, and ask questions until you are satisfied that you understand the right answers for you.

You have the power to come out on top, if only you know how to use it. Regardless of your starting point, you can become a debt master.

There Are New Answers for a New Era

The old rules and ways of managing money and debt won't work, but there are new ones that will. In this book, you will learn about new products and services like these:

- **Truth in Equity,** a company that can show you how to pay off your mortgage in five to seven years without making higher mortgage payments.
- **Healthcare Advocates,** a firm that will negotiate with your doctors and hospitals to cut your medical costs down to affordable levels.
- **Credit Karma,** a company that will let you monitor your credit score for free, and teach you how to improve it.
- **Income-based repayment,** new plans from the Department of Education that will keep your student loans affordable while you pursue volunteer work, push through unemployment, or enter a low-paying career.

And so on. I've scoured the Web, I've worked my sources, and I've networked with hundreds of financial professionals and organizations to pull out the best and the brightest strategies for the new era of debt.

Know this: You can get out of debt. You can pay less than you thought possible for leverage or debt. You can get credit card companies to pay you, instead of the other way around. You can burn your mortgage before you send your kids to college, and keep their borrowing to a minimum once they get there. I'll show you how to take it one step at a time.

A Word about My Favorite Secret

One of the strategies revealed in this book is called "equity accelera-tion." This is not the biweekly mortgage payment plans you might have read about years ago. This is a new way of managing your family money that could help you to get completely debt free in less than a decade *and* change the way you manage your money forever.

It is so innovative that I asked its chief proponent, Bill Westrom of Truth in Equity, to help me with that chapter of the book. I'll say no more about it now—check out Chapter 6!

How to Approach This Book

Consider this book the first tool to use in your debt mastery program. You can use it in the way that works best for you.

If you want to rebuild your debt life and use of credit from start to finish, you should read the book from start to finish; I've arranged the chapters so that the first part of the book creates the foundation for the rest of the book.

If you already feel like you are drowning in debt, go directly to Chapter 10, where I've located most of the emergency advice that is in this book. There you will find advice on how to dig out, which bills to pay, and how to hold on to your home. After you've looked that over, you can return to Chapter 1 and read the rest of the book in order.

If there's one kind of debt that's at the top of your to-do list now, you can go directly to the chapter that deals with those particular issues. There are, for example, chapters about student loans, car loans, and mortgages.

Here's an overview of how the book is organized.

Chapter 1: How Did We Get Here? And Where Are We? This chapter includes an overview of the credit crisis that hit late in this decade, as well as a survey of the current debt landscape.

Chapter 2: Find Out Where You Stand. You can't dig out of debt until you know where you are. Here are worksheets and exercises to get you started on a whole new debt plan.

Chapter 3: Other People Are Grading You, Too. Credit reports and scores aren't what they used to be. How to keep your file clean, build a top credit score, and avoid the scammers hiding in this business.

Chapter 4: Avoiding a Modern-Day Identity Crisis. Protecting your good name means protecting your credit. Identity fraud has grown exponentially, but this chapter reveals how to make sure it doesn't happen to you.

Chapter 5: Win the New Mortgage Game. Forget the crazy mortgages of the previous decade. This chapter shows how to secure the money you need for your home, get a good refi, burn a bad mortgage, and get out from under years of payments sooner than you ever thought possible.

Chapter 6: Mortgage Free in Five to Seven Years. This revolutionary strategy may change the way you pay every bill for the rest of your life, and put hundreds of thousands of extra dollars in your pocket.

Chapter 7: Credit Cards: Just Because It's Called MasterCard Doesn't Mean It's the Boss of You. All that you need to know now about credit cards. How to get the best deals without falling into the rate traps. New rules from Washington.

Chapter 8: Car Deals: Making Sure You're in the Driver's Seat. Zero percent car loans aren't so easy to find anymore, and they often cost more than they are worth, anyway. How to get the best bottom-line deal on your car, and how to pay for it.

Chapter 9: An Education in College Costs. The entire student loan landscape is dramatically different today. How to get the money you need for college, when and how to borrow, and how to pay it off so student debt doesn't destroy your future.

Chapter 10: Don't Let Bad Luck Derail Your Finances. This is the chapter for anyone who's in debt trouble. Don't worry, take action. This is where you will find the groups that can help, the negotiations that can make a difference, and the strategies that will get you out of debt quickly and cleanly. What to do about a health emergency, how to reduce your medical debts, and how to modify your mortgage and avoid foreclosure.

Chapter 11: Surviving Bankruptcy. A clean guide through the worst-case scenarios, and even they aren't as bad as you think. How to manage bankruptcy or foreclosure and come out whole on the other side.

Chapter 12: Debt Strategies for Every Age. What works when you're 15 years old isn't a good idea at 50, and vice versa. A handy checklist for debt mastery at any age.

Chapter 13: Permanent Mastery, Going Forward. The rules of the road for the future. How to manage debt and money when the financial marketplace changes again. You know it will.

Appendix: Resources.

I'd like to say something about the extensive resource list at the end of the book.

One of the most important skills involved in managing money is knowing whom to listen to. Unfortunately, there are fewer and fewer really strong, really dedicated, and really independent financial advisers out there for everyday consumers. Too many so-called experts are simply selling products. Others are nonprofit and may have their hearts in the right place, but they are being starved of necessary funds. It's harder to find solid sources of good information.

Consumer education has been my calling for my entire professional life. But I don't claim to know everything, and I don't claim to have been able to fit everything I do know into this handy little book. So, I have included a generous list of good resources in most chapters and at the end of the book.

These are resources that offer solid information or services that can help you find the answers you need, do the math, and plot the strategies that you will need going forward. I have worked very hard to screen the organizations and experts that I recommend, and I have faith in their expertise, their dedication, and their ability to supplement the information in this book and help you on the road to debt mastery.

1

How Did We Get Here?
And Where Are We?

We haven't ever been here before. The debt landscape has changed dramatically and irrevocably, and the ways in which we borrowed, spent, and repaid debts before are relics of the past.

The cash-back credit card offers that used to crowd our mailboxes have dried up.

There's no such thing as a "No down payment? No problem!" mortgage.

Those tempting teaser rates are long gone, replaced by "gotcha" interest costs so high you'd think the Mob was involved.

It's sometimes impossible to borrow money at any price—for college, a car, or a home renovation. And you need to submit a credit card at the front desk before a doctor will even see you now.

It may seem like credit has dried up altogether, just when you need it the most.

What hasn't disappeared is the debt. American consumers are on the hook for close to $3 trillion, not counting their mortgages, according to the Federal Reserve. The average credit card holder is juggling almost $11,000 in debt on close to 13 cards. Roughly one of every three homeowners is underwater, meaning that they owe more on their homes than the homes are worth.

And paybacks are rough. As banks and other lenders began pulling back on credit, they tightened terms and squeezed indebted consumers. Interest rates skyrocketed, and so did minimum monthly payments on everything from credit cards to mortgages.

1

Middle-class people who were barely making it aren't making it anymore. Those in the worst situations are trapped in houses they can't afford to pay for and are unable to sell. Others are selling homes at bargain-basement prices and downsizing. Or sending their kids to community colleges instead of the private colleges they were aiming for. Or working nights and weekends and skipping lunch to make the payments on their MasterCard and Visa bills.

And yet, all is far from lost. If there were no good news, there would be no reason for this book. I'd just crawl back into bed and call it a day—or a decade.

But there *is* good news. In the first place, the dialing back of debt in the United States was necessary. As a society, we got overextended. Now, there's a renewed feeling of responsibility in the air as banks and consumers ratchet back to a more sustainable and stable way of doing business. The federal government has stepped in, over and over again, to tighten standards of behavior for creditors and to protect the borrowing public. There are more ways to protect your home, your family, and your credit score than there were a year or two ago.

And, as has always happened in U.S. economic history, the marketplace is adapting to the new era with new products and services for consumers. Some of them are shoddy, or worse. But many offer new and innovative ways to manage debt.

That's why we're here. With the right information and the right techniques, you can take charge of your debts, blow them away, and prosper. You can negotiate with your credit card issuer, rework your mortgage, and improve your credit score so you qualify for the lowest-cost, best deals out there.

You can pay off your mortgage years—and thousands of dollars—early. You can still find credit card issuers that pay you back. You can get more cash out of your child's first-choice school that you don't have to pay back.

I will show you how.

But first, it's instructive to see how we got here.

A Long Time Coming

Americans have had a long love affair with debt, but it really rose to prominence in the 1980s and 1990s. The deregulation of financial institutions meant that there were many more lenders competing for borrowers and that they faced fewer rules about their interest rates and practices.

More debt became securitized—bundled up and resold to investors. Mortgage-backed securities were the most common of these arrangements, and they resulted in mortgage-backed mutual funds for investors and a big, steady stream of cash for mortgage lenders. As everything from auto loans to credit cards got securitized, that meant more money coming back to banks and other issuers so they could quickly turn around and lend it to new borrowers. This also served to separate the lenders from the ultimate holders of the debt: Banks that issued mortgages weren't holding on to them; they were selling them off as fast as they could issue them.

At the same time, the credit scoring business was growing up. This gave lenders quick numerical answers to their questions about the creditworthiness of customers. Instead of poring over credit reports for hours, they could get a score in moments that would qualify a borrower as a good prospect.

Here's what happened when all of that came together: Lenders that issued mortgages, car loans, student loans, and even credit card accounts were able to make money fast by qualifying a borrower, collecting a fee (or, more typically, a lot of fees), and then selling the loan off to someone else. The lenders didn't even really care whether the borrower made good on the loan; they only cared about the borrower looking good enough to qualify in the first place.

As interest rates fell in the 1990s, refinancing became another popular way for lenders to make money, over and over again, from the same homeowners. They encouraged people to do cash-out refinance deals—borrow against the swelling equity in their homes to pay off other debts, improve their homes, send their kids to college, and do anything else that struck their fancy.

By 2005, the country was in the midst of a housing bubble, and would-be homeowners were told they should do whatever it took to buy a house before it was too late and they couldn't afford it any more. Some lenders simply allowed themselves to be pressured by brokers, real estate agents, homeowners, and their own bosses to make more and more loans. But some particularly unethical predatory lenders went out of their way to push cash-out refinance deals on unqualified, unsuspecting, and naive (often elderly) homeowners who gave up good, small, inexpensive loans for subprime deals that turned out to be disasters.

The creative folks in the mortgage and real estate industries did what they could to invent new mortgages that would allow more and more borrowers to qualify. There were new mortgages that required no down payment and no demonstrable income from borrowers. They started with teaser rates, tiny monthly payments and a feeling of euphoria. But they held deadly traps, like interest rates that reset at levels that doubled and tripled monthly payments, and amortization schedules calculated so that the balance of the loans grew over time instead of shrinking.

While that was happening, everything from college to cars was becoming less and less affordable. College costs were rising precipitously, and neither household income nor government aid programs were growing quite as fast. Lenders rushed into that void, too—creating a student loan industry that was predatory in its own way. At its worst, it was found to be kicking money back to schools that were recommending costly private loans to students who had been told that no price was too high for a good education. Those loans carried an implicit college seal of approval that made students and their parents think they were good deals.

As cars became unaffordable, dealers and manufacturers cooked up auto loans that stretched longer than the useful lives of the sport utility vehicles they were paying for. It became possible to get a seven-year car loan, and it was not unusual for car owners to trade in their cars before their loans were paid off. They were adding the balances of their old loans to their new car loans.

Credit cards became as common as head colds, and issuers who could now qualify borrowers and process payments for pennies went crazy promoting the cards. Every store and affinity group, from sports clubs to hamburger joints, had its own card. To encourage consumers to use the cards for even the tiniest pack-of-gum type purchases, issuers started promoting the cards with big cash-back bonuses for money charged at gas stations, convenience stores, and groceries. Then they started piling on the fees. Issuers that used to depend on interest income and fees from merchants discovered they could really cash in if they charged consumers for being late, for going over their credit limits, for getting cash advances, and for anything else they could think of.

Borrowers did their part, buying into more and more debt for any and every reason, and thinking it was all okay. By 2006, the United States had a negative savings rate for the entire year. That means—and it bears repeating—that as a nation, on average, all Americans were spending more than they made, borrowing to make up the difference. Consumer debt quintupled between 1980 and 2001, and then practically doubled again to $2.6 trillion in 2008.

Pop! It had to happen. The credit spree that had taken decades to build came to a crashing halt in 2007. It started when the lowest tier of mortgage borrowers—those folks who'd been talked into crazy mortgages—stopped being able to keep up with the rising monthly payments. The investors who held big portfolios of weak loans didn't have the cash to float new loans. The bankers stopped making money. Housing prices started to fall, and people weren't able to refinance, pull money out of their homes, or even get new loans for new homes. Prices fell further. The banks, worried about where the next shoe was going to drop, started pulling back on consumer debt. They cut credit lines on home equity lines and on credit cards. Consumers lost their borrowing ability and their breathing room. Stocks got slammed, and it all started spiraling downward. Joblessness, bankruptcies, delinquencies, and interest rates were on the rise, and spirits, paychecks, and economic activity dropped.

The government stepped in, on almost a dozen different occasions. In the fall of 2007, President George W. Bush created the Hope Now Alliance, a union of mortgage investors (including giants Fannie Mae and Freddie Mac), the Federal Housing Administration, mortgage lenders, and trade groups. The group was to provide free counseling and voluntary workout assistance to troubled borrowers. In September 2007, Congress passed, and President Bush signed, the College Cost Reduction and Access Act, which cut interest rates on federal college loans and eased repayment options for struggling graduates.

Early in 2008, Congress enacted the Economic Stimulus Act of 2008, legislation that put an additional $600 into the hands of most taxpayers quickly. That wasn't enough, though, to address the systemic problems that worsened throughout the year. In July 2008, under President Bush, Congress passed the Housing and Economic Recovery Act of 2008, designed to ease credit in the mortgage markets and make more cash available to support refinance loans for sub-prime borrowers. The Higher Education Opportunity Act was passed by Congress and signed by President Bush in the summer of 2008. In February 2009, President Barack Obama and Congress approved the

American Recovery and Reinvestment Act of 2009. This was a grab bag of provisions, including money for students, car buyers, and homeowners. In March 2009, the Obama administration unveiled a comprehensive mortgage relief plan called "Making Home Afford-able." In subsequent months, it refined and amended that program. Later in 2009, Congress passed, and President Obama signed, a comprehensive credit card reform bill.

A New Era

Now we are digesting all of this. As a nation, we are moving out of recession and into a new economic era. We are adjusting to the new benefits, rules, and programs that came out of that mountain of legislation. As consumers, we are learning to take advantage of the new programs while learning to live without the easy money that used to be all around us. That's not so bad—the money really wasn't that easy after all.

In the following pages, I'll take you through all that is new about managing debt in the United States, circa 2010 and beyond. We'll discuss every unique type of debt, from credit cards to mortgages, in great detail. I'll show you where the traps are hidden and where the great new opportunities lie.

For starters, here is a quick overview of the major types of debts that most Americans deal with, along with the recent changes and trends in each area.

- **Mortgages.** The biggest and most important debt for most Americans, mortgages have changed dramatically, and changed again. Now we are in an era when mortgages are moving back to more traditional forms—plain-vanilla, 30-year fixed-rate mortgages dominate the marketplace. There are still some variable-rate mortgages.

    Mortgages are secured loans—they are backed by the property on which they are written.

    There are two new government-backed programs for mort-gage holders who are in trouble. One allows homeowners to refinance their homes, even if the homes are worth less than their loans. A second one encourages mortgage lenders to modify mortgages for troubled borrowers by lowering interest rates and payments.

- **Home equity lines of credit (HELOCs).** These lines of credit are backed by your home, and give you a lot of control over your money. You can use them to fund renovations, buy cars, pay bills, and more, and repay them on your own schedule, as long as you are making monthly minimum payments as big as your monthly interest costs. Disciplined homeowners can really make their HELOCs work for them by using the equity accelerator technique described later in this book. You can use a HELOC to burn your mortgage faster than you ever thought possible.

  Bankers tend to like home equity lines, too; they don't typically resell them, so the loans stay in bank portfolios, producing cash flow. There are still many HELOCs on the market, and competition from lenders wanting to place HELOCs with homeowners.

- **Reverse mortgages.** These products put money in the hands of elderly homeowners in exchange for repayment when the home is sold. They used to be prohibitively expensive, and they still can carry some high fees, but they have been improving. They work best in very specialized situations. An older person who is not well and doesn't want to leave home can use a reverse mortgage to pay for care. A reverse mortgage typically reduces the amount of equity that heirs inherit.

- **Credit cards.** It's almost impossible to live without credit cards now, but they have gotten more complicated than ever. Consumers who carry credit card debt balances—about half of all cardholders—are at the mercy of card issuers that have been jacking up rates and fees as aggressively and unconscionably as I've seen in my decades-long career.

  New government rules slated to go into effect in 2010 will limit issuers' ability to retroactively raise rates and trap consumers into late payment charges. Many in the industry say issuers will stop offering generous cash-back deals and start charging annual fees. Those moves may make it harder for the half of consumers who pay off their bills every month to really profit from credit card use, but there is still enough competition in that space to make me think you'll have some good choices for a while.

- **Car loans.** The typical car loan has gotten longer and costlier over the years, but troubled automakers are making amends with price cuts that may outweigh the zero percent financing offers that used to rule. Washington has been offering its own incentives; in 2009 it offered a sales tax credit to car buyers. Congress also enacted a "cash for clunkers" incentive for car buyers who turn in old, gas-guzzling cars. Lease deals, which used to be prohibitively expensive, now sometimes rival car loans as a less expensive way to buy a car.

- **Installment loans.** When stores offer no-interest-for-a-year deals, or agree to finance your TV, computer, or new living room furniture, that's an installment loan. They can be pretty pricey, and rarely are the best way to pay for a purchase. The no-interest promotions have largely dried up; those that remain usually are carefully constructed to trap the borrower into paying interest. You have to monitor them very carefully. Some medical offices are now offering their own installment loans, usually for high-priced procedures that insurance doesn't cover, such as LASIK eye surgery or cosmetic surgery.

- **Student loans.** The way in which families pay for college is shifting dramatically. That's a good thing. In the late 1990s and early 2000s, increased dependence on costly private loans put some graduates into so much debt they had to give up on favored careers and grad school. Now the federal government is the direct, primary lender for a much larger share of student loans, and rates have come down. There's a host of new repayment plans that offer great leniency to students who graduate and enter low-paying public service careers.

- **Retirement plan and life insurance loans.** You can borrow money from yourself. Many companies allow workers to borrow against their own 401(k) accounts; in those cases the interest you pay back is paid into your own account. Most advisers do not recommend this strategy; it removes money from an account you should allow to grow until you retire. But this can actually be a reasonable place to borrow money in an emergency; it costs less than some other forms of debt.

  Cash-value life insurance policies also allow account holders to borrow their own money back. This, too, can be a reasonable way to meet emergency expenses or even pay for college or other big costs, especially if you no longer need the full life insurance death benefit.

Other Kinds of Loans

There are a couple of other categories not discussed in this book—payday loans and tax refund anticipation loans, for example. I do not consider either legitimate enough to include in a book about debt mastery; you can't be the master of a sleazy product that preys on the poorest in society and charges fees and rates that can approach 500 percent on an annual basis. Just avoid them both; that's all there is to say about them.

I also haven't discussed margin loans in this book. Those are funds that investors borrow to pay for bets they make on stocks, bonds, and commodities. They are very risky indeed, and best left for an investment book and not a debt book.

But except for those examples, the earlier list includes all of the types of loans and debt that most Americans contend with. Each has its advantages and disadvantages, its own pitfalls and rewards.

You may use them all at different times of your life. To truly master them, to take the greatest advantage of each type of loan, to snag the lowest rates, to keep your payments manageable, and to get yourself completely free of debt when you need to be, you'll have to be both disciplined and determined. But first, you'll have to start at the beginning, by figuring out exactly where you stand.

CHAPTER

2

Find Out Where You Stand

If I had only one bit of advice to share—my number one, most important piece of financial advice after a lifetime of giving financial advice—it would be this:

Don't lie to yourself about your money.

You're lying to yourself if you don't know how much money you owe, or what the interest rate is on your credit card, or what your house is worth right now. Maybe the financial truths are painful—you are afraid to look at all of your debts at once. Or maybe they're just burdensome and confusing, so you go through every month getting paid and paying bills without looking at the big picture. Maybe you're comfortable financially, so you don't want to bother putting the time into studying your entire financial situation.

Those are all different ways of hiding from the truth about your money, and they are all self-defeating and painful.

Wherever you are right now, I promise you that you can absolutely, positively improve your financial situation. But only if you know where you are right now. You need a starting point, and you need to be absolutely honest with yourself about where you stand.

That means you need to pull together all of your financial records and perform the following assessments:

- A net worth statement
- A cash flow statement
- A risk test
- A debt analysis

By the time you've done the work of this chapter, you'll have a very firm foundation for improving your finances, making the most of your credit, and managing your debt. And you'll feel better— getting a firm grasp of your financial situation is like taking a shower or cleaning out the closets. It's a fresh start.

Financial Management Programs

I've included some worksheets in this book, just to keep everything contained and simple. But in this computerized age, you should probably be using a personal finance program to keep track of your money. Invest the time and effort into entering your financial life into a program, and going forward you will have push-button answers to all of the questions posed in this chapter. You will know, at any moment, how much you are worth, and you will see the immediate impact of making an extra payment on your car loan or into your retirement fund. You'll be able to determine how much you're spending on groceries and insurance. You'll be able to always be on top of your finances. It will make planning easier, and save you money and time at tax time.

There are two types of financial programs available now: desktop programs and Web-based aggregators.

1. **Desktop programs.** These are software programs you can load onto your computer. You can usually download transaction information from your banks and brokers into the program, so once you've set up accounts, you shouldn't have to type in any transactions. These programs keep track of your entire financial life, including your investments, loans, bills, and checking account balances. The two market leaders are:

   • Quicken, from Intuit, available at www.quicken.com.
   • Microsoft MoneyPlus, from Microsoft, available at www.microsoft. com/money.

2. **Web-based aggregators.** There's a new generation of financial management software available, usually for free, online. These sites aggregate data from your various accounts; you essentially give the programs the authority and passwords they need to pull information from your credit cards and bank accounts, and they assemble all of the data in one place, so you can sign in and see up-to-date information about exactly where your money is and how you are spending it.

Most of these sites add the extra wrinkle of social networking: They include advice and tips from other site members who might have similar financial profiles to you, or who might shop at the same places. The advantages of these sites are that they are accessible from anywhere, and they take almost no effort on your part to keep up to date. Not all of them include investment accounts, so they are less helpful if you want a full-featured program. However, that makes them simpler to use if you just want to track your expenses. Some of the leaders are:

* Buxfer, www.buxfer.com
* Green Sherpa, www.greensherpa.com
* Mint, www.mint.com
* Money Strands, www.moneystrands.com
* Quicken Online, www.quicken.com
* Wesabe, www.wesabe.com

Take a few hours to surf around each one, look at the demos, and decide which approach you're most comfortable with. They offer very similar features but are designed differently.

First, Determine Your Net Worth

Your net worth is a snapshot of your financial standing. It's a simple formula of everything you owe subtracted from everything you own. If you owe more than you own, you're in the red. If you own more than you owe, you're in the black.

To determine your net worth, list all of your assets—what you own. And then subtract all of your liabilities—what you owe. You can use the following worksheet. Even though everything you own—such as your clothes and your big-screen TV—are assets, it is not worth including them in this calculation. Unless something is of significant value and you can or would sell it, don't bother putting it here.

Net Worth Worksheet

Current Assets	Value
Checking account	_____
Savings account	_____
Money market funds	_____

Savings bonds   _____
Certificates of deposit   _____
Health care savings account   _____
Subtotal, current assets   _____

Investments	**Value**
Stocks	_____
Mutual funds	_____
Bonds	_____
Subtotal, investments	_____

Real Estate Assets	**Value**
Your house	_____
Second home	_____
Other real estate	_____
Subtotal, real estate assets	_____

Long-Term Assets	**Value**
Annuities	_____
IRAs	_____
Life insurance cash value	_____
401(k), 403(b), or 457 plan	_____
Self-employed retirement plan	_____
Other	_____
Subtotal, long-term assets	_____

Personal Property	**Value**
Antiques	_____
Cars	_____
Jewelry	_____
Collectibles	_____
Other (cars, boats)	_____
Subtotal, personal property	_____
Total assets	_____

Current Liabilities	**Value**
Credit card balances	_____
Money owed to individuals	_____
Medical debts	_____
Bank line of credit	_____
Subtotal, current liabilities	_____

Real Estate Liabilities	**Value**
Home #1	
First mortgage	_____
Second mortgage	_____

Home equity line balance	_____
Home #2	
First mortgage	_____
Second mortgage	_____
Home equity line balance	_____
Rental property	
First mortgage	_____
Second mortgage	_____
Home equity line balance	_____
Subtotal, real estate liabilities	_____

Long-Term Liabilities	**Value**
Car loan balances	_____
Education loan balances	_____
Home improvement loans	_____
Loans against 401(k), 403(b), or 457 plans	_____
Loans against life insurance	_____
Other installment loans	_____
Subtotal, long-term liabilities	_____
Total liabilities	_____
Net worth (Total assets – Total liabilities)	_____

Now that you've taken the time to account for everything on that chart, you know a lot. You know your total net worth, and I hope it is a positive number. That means you've already been keeping your debt in check and growing your assets. But even if it is a negative number, don't worry too much; in later chapters you'll learn how to turn that around.

You know some other things as well. You can look at your list of assets and liabilities and see if they stack up. Are all of your assets in short-term (current) accounts, while your loans are long-term? Do you owe more on real estate (or cars) than you own? Is all of your money locked up in long-term investments, but you have a lot of short-term liabilities? These are all mismatches that you will be able to correct, as you move forward. You've already done the important step of identifying them.

Keeping track of your net worth over time can also teach you a lot about how your whole financial life works. Your net worth statement is a snapshot of a reality that is constantly changing. Every time you pay a credit card bill, or deposit your paycheck, or see the share prices of your mutual funds go up or down, your net worth is changing along with that action. For bottom-line purposes, paying off $100 in credit card debt has the exact same impact on your net worth as a $100 increase in the value of your IRA or getting a $100 check for your birthday from Grandma. Of course there are reasons why sometimes one is better than another, and you'll learn the finer points of this later in the book. But for now, just studying your net worth tells you a lot.

Analyze Your Cash Flow

Your net worth may change all the time, but it doesn't really show you where your money comes from and where it goes. For that, you need a budget or cash flow statement. A cash flow statement will subtract all of your expenses from all of your income. If the number at the bottom is positive, you know you are getting ahead. If it is negative, you are digging yourself deeper into debt every month.

This can be really hard to create if you're just thinking about this for the first time. Most people have a big "miscellaneous" category that throws off their best attempts to record their expenses (and save money). But fill in the following worksheet to the best of your ability, and promise yourself to spend a couple of weeks recording *all* of your expenses so you can fill in the blanks.

Cash Flow Worksheet

You can use monthly figures or annual figures to fill this out; just make sure you are consistent all the way down. If you're filling out a monthly worksheet, make sure you include bills you may only pay annually, such as your property taxes, divided by 12.

Income

Earned Income	Amount
Salary—your job	_____
Salary—spouse's job	_____
Salary—other jobs	_____
Bonuses	_____
Tips	_____
Subtotal, earned income	_____

Self-Employed Income	Amount
Freelance or hobby income	_____
Real estate rental income	_____

EBay sales, etc.   _____
Small business income   _____
Subtotal, self-employed income   _____

Other Income	**Amount**
Government benefits	_____
Gifts from relatives	_____
Child support or alimony	_____
Disability insurance income	_____
Family trust income	_____
Inheritance income	_____
Subtotal, other income	_____

Retirement Income	**Amount**
Annuity payments	_____
Social Security income	_____
Pension income	_____
401(k) withdrawals	_____
IRA withdrawals	_____
Subtotal, retirement income	_____

Investment Income	**Amount**
Bank account interest	_____
Bond interest	_____
Stock dividends	_____
Bond fund distributions	_____
Mutual fund dividends	_____
Capital gains	_____
Subtotal, investment income	_____
Total income	_____

Expenses

Fixed Expenses	**Amount**
Alimony	_____
Car payments	_____
Child support	_____
Mortgage payments	_____
Rent	_____
Condo fees	_____
Insurance premiums	
Auto	_____
Dental	_____

Disability   _____
Health   _____
Homeowner's   _____
Life   _____
Utilities
   Gas   _____
   Oil   _____
   Electric   _____
   Water   _____
   Cable TV   _____
   Phone   _____
   Internet   _____
   Cell phone   _____
School tuition   _____
Church or synagogue dues   _____
Income taxes, federal   _____
Income taxes, state and local   _____
401(k), 403(b), or 457 plan contributions   _____
Property taxes   _____
Other fixed expenses   _____
Subtotal, fixed expenses   _____

Flexible Expenses	**Amount**
Children's activities	_____
Clothing	_____
Charitable contributions	_____
Gifts	_____
Groceries	_____
Medical bills	_____
Prescription drugs	_____
Dental bills	_____
Personal care (haircuts, etc.)	_____
Magazines, newspapers	_____
Pet care	_____
Hobbies	_____
Movies, entertainment	_____
Dining out	_____
Vacations	_____
Home maintenance	_____
Fees for financial advice	_____
Furniture, electronics, etc.	_____
Garden supplies	_____
Yard maintenance	_____
Savings—emergency fund	_____

Mystery cash	_____
Other	_____
Subtotal, flexible expenses	_____
Total expenses	_____
Total net cash flow (Total income – Total expenses)	_____

Now you know a whole lot more. You know whether you have any discretionary income at all or all of your funds are being completely eaten up by expenses. You may even see a few spots, under the flexible expenses category, where you could save money if you really wanted to or had to. Over time, you will be able to fine-tune this worksheet as you see where your money really goes. You may add or subtract some categories of your own. If your total net cash flow is positive, and you've been realistic about all of your expenses, you're in great shape—you can plow more money into saving and investing or use it to pay down costly debt quickly. If you're earning less than you're spending, you've got some work to do. But now you can see the size of your problem.

Do a Risk Test

Do you remember in 2009 when the federal government subjected all of the big banks to stress tests? Basically, all they were doing was checking to see if the banks had adequate emergency resources to make it through a variety of worst-case scenarios.

You should do the same thing with your own family finances. Sit down with your net worth worksheet and your cash flow worksheet, and ask yourself these questions:

- If I lost my job, how many months would I be able to keep up with my bills?
- If my car or my roof failed today, how would I pay to replace it?
- If someone in my family got sick, how would we cover those expenses?
- If my investments lost 35 percent of their value, could I still retire?

You can and should make up other questions based on your own situation. For example, if you own rental property, you could ask, "How will I make ends meet if my tenants move out?"

Use the answers to your risk test to lay the groundwork for a firmer foundation. Sometimes, the answers will point you to buying more insurance, or beefing up that emergency fund so that you have six months of living expenses stashed at the bank. Sometimes there's no easy answer, and the question exposes a vulnerability in your financial plan. But that is good to know, too.

Analyze Your Debts

And now we come to the analysis that is most fundamental to this book: the analysis of your debts.

Like any good chief financial officer, you should make sure that your use of credit works for your lifestyle and your goals. You should make sure you're borrowing in safe amounts, with good loans that don't cost too much.

You should have already listed all of your debts when you were preparing your net worth statement, but now you should look a little bit closer. Write down again all of your debts on the following debt worksheet, including additional information, such as when you took out the loan. For every debt you have, you should also list the original balance and opening date, the maturity date, the minimum monthly payment, the interest rate, whether the rate is variable or fixed, whether there is a prepayment penalty for paying it off early, and whether the interest on the debt is tax deductible. You can add other rows if you have additional accounts.

Now, with all of your debts listed, you can start to analyze them to see how they stack up. Here are eight ways to measure whether your debts are good ones or they need restructuring.

1. Are your loan rates competitive? Compare the interest rates you are paying against market averages now. You can find current rates for just about any type of loan at the Bankrate web site (www.bankrate.com). If you are paying above-average rates for any of your loans, you'll want to think about refinancing that debt or paying it off early.
2. Do you have credit card balances? That's almost always a negative. If you have balances on more than one card, there are some good strategies for paying them off in sequence. Go to Chapter 7 to learn more about that.

Debt Worksheet

Debt	Date Opened	Original Balance	Current Balance	Maturity Date	Monthly Payment	Interest Rate (Variable or Fixed)	Prepayment Penalty	Tax Deductible
Mortgage								
Second mortgage								
Mortgage (second home)								
Home equity line								
Auto loan								
Second auto loan								
Student loan								
Installment loan								
Personal loan								
401(k) loan								
Insurance loan								
Credit card #1								
Credit card #2								
Other debts								

3. Are you getting a tax break on your debts? The interest on most home mortgages and home equity lines is tax deductible, but there are some limitations on this. The details are in Chapter 5.

4. Are you too vulnerable to rate increases? Interest rates recently have been near their historic lows, especially for mortgages. But if you have some loans (or many loans) with variable interest rates, you could really get slammed if rates rise as the economy strengthens. You may want to lock in fixed rates now, or at least plan for the possibility of higher monthly payments going forward.

5. Is all of your debt secured or unsecured? A secured debt is one that is backed by collateral. Your car loan is secured by your car, for example, and if you stopped making payments on it, someone would eventually come to your house and repossess your car. It's good to have secured debt, because the collateral results in lower interest rates. But it's not good if all of your debt is secured. Credit cards, for example, are not secured, and that is one reason why their rates are so high. But if a crisis

strikes and you end up defaulting on some of your debt, it would be nice to know your house isn't on the line.

6. Are you a big revolver? Fixed-term loans, such as most car loans and mortgages, have a definite end date when, if you make the required monthly payments, you'll have paid the loan in full. Credit cards and home equity lines of credit are different. They revolve, meaning that you can carry a balance from month to month and make minimum payments and borrow new money and get a new balance and *never* pay off the loan. That can come in handy if you have big cash flow issues. For example, if you're self-employed and your income is very volatile, you can use the open-endedness of the revolving account to smooth your cash flow. But the ability to do so usually comes at a high cost, in terms of interest paid. Many installment loans, such as the loan you get from the furniture company to pay for that bedroom set, are also revolving.

7. Are you making the most of all this borrowing power? This is a complex question, but before debt got a bad name in the recent credit meltdown it was sometimes called leverage. If you can borrow other people's money at low interest rates and use it to buy a good home for your family, to start a business, or to gain an education, that's not a bad thing. But if your listed debts have mainly gotten you meals you've already digested or toys you've already broken, you may want to rethink the way you use your borrowing power.

8. Is there an end in sight when your debts will be paid off? It's usually not a good idea to carry too much debt into retirement. It's especially important to pay off 401(k), 403(b), or 457 loans before you need to start drawing on your 401(k) and the like. If you have mortgage debt, credit card debt, and other loans as far as the eye can see, you may want to focus your finances on paying back those loans more quickly than they demand. It's a good idea to match up loan maturities with anticipated lifestyle events. For example, if you know you'll be shopping for education loans in four years, you may want to make sure your car is paid off by then. If you're still paying off an installment loan you took out for your daughter's wedding, you may want to make sure it's paid off before you want to start putting money away for your first grandchild's education.

Are You in Trouble?

Finally, there's one more question you have to ask about your debts. Are there too many of them? If your monthly debt payments, including mortgages and credit cards, take up more than 36 percent of your gross monthly income, you've probably got too much debt. Payments on all of your debts excluding your mortgage should be 20 percent or less of your monthly pay. If just seeing all of your debts listed in one place makes you queasy, you may have more debt than your income can support.

There are ways to fix that, too, and I outline them later in the book. But for now, take a hard look at all of the worksheets you've created in this chapter and look at the warning signs listed next to determine whether you have a serious problem with debt. If you do, go straight to Chapter 10, the "Bad Luck" chapter, and read about how to fix your troubles.

Warning Signs of Debt Problems

- You juggle your bills, paying one company one month and another the next.
- You frequently receive overdue notices.
- You make only minimum payments on your revolving loans.
- You've reached your limits on most or all of your credit cards and lines of credit.
- You are borrowing money for everyday necessities like food and gasoline, and then failing to pay it off at the end of the month.
- You regularly overdraw your checking account.
- You use one line of credit to pay another. For example, you write a check on your home equity line to make your car payment.
- You didn't know (until you did these worksheets) how much you were spending on interest.
- You lose sleep worrying about bills.
- You don't have an emergency fund.
- As soon as you pay off your credit card, you charge it up again.
- You've been denied credit recently.
- Sometimes, you just don't open your bills because it's too painful.

. . . Which brings us back to my number one rule: Don't lie to yourself about your money. Instead, pat yourself on the back for going through all of the rigorous exercises in this chapter. Now you know where you stand, you've identified the strengths and the weak spots, and you're ready to start managing your debt so that it works for you, instead of the other way around. Good job, and an excellent first step.

CHAPTER 3

Other People Are Grading You, Too

You aren't the only one looking over your finances. Your financial behavior is an open book that banks, lenders, merchants, and credit bureaus are studying carefully.

They know all about you. They know how many credit cards you have, and whether you pay your bills on time. They know how often you've moved, where you work, and whether you're married, divorced, or single. They know if you tend to carry balances on your cards or pay them off every month. They share all of those details with each other, and use that information to grade you. Then they use those grades to decide how to treat you in the marketplace.

To qualify for the loans you want and to get the best interest rates, you have to understand how you are graded and you have to make sure you're being graded fairly and accurately. You have to know how to bump up those grades if they aren't high enough. Here is what you need to know about credit reports and credit scores.

A *credit report* is a history of your credit behavior. It includes all of your open (and closed) mortgages, credit cards, and other loans. It also includes personal data, such as your address and Social Security number. The three credit reporting bureaus, Equifax, Experian, and TransUnion, keep and maintain credit reports for everyone who has ever borrowed money.

A *credit score* is a single three-digit number, calculated when a company takes all of the information in your credit report and runs it through a private mathematical formula. Credit scores are increasingly being used as predictors of creditworthiness and risk.

In the past decade or so, credit scoring has exploded, and so has the use of credit. When lenders realized they could simply look at one three-digit number to decide whether to give you a credit card (and how high your interest rate should be), the use of scoring went wild. So did all of those prequalified credit card mailings.

Along the way, some consumers got trampled. Mistakes in their credit files and disputes with merchants led to problems in their credit reports and bad credit scores. Consumers had trouble getting copies of their files, and even more trouble fixing problems, even though the Fair Credit Reporting Act, designed to protect consumers' rights in this area, had been on the books since 1970.

The feds stepped in, in 2003, with the Fair and Accurate Credit Transactions Act (FACTA) of 2003. It secured consumers' rights to get free access to their credit reports, and also gave them the power to limit how others see and use their reports. I'll give you more details about that later in this chapter and in Chapter 4, when I talk about how to protect yourself from identity theft.

Ironically, when Congress gave consumers free access to their credit reports, it led to the development of a whole new industry: companies offering a host of credit monitoring and credit scoring services to consumers who aren't sure how to view or manage their reports and their scores. You absolutely have to check and manage your reports and your scores at some times, but you don't have to be scared into buying every credit checking product that comes down the pike, makes up a catchy jingle, and advertises heavily on television. Here's how to manage your credit files and scores.

How Credit Reports Work

There are three national credit reporting companies—Equifax, Experian, and TransUnion. They know all about you, you should know about them. They get reports about you from the lenders you do business with, especially auto lenders and credit card issuers, including banks and also retailers like Macy's and Home Depot. Mortgages and other debts, such as utility bills and doctor bills, are typically not reported to the credit reporting companies unless you are habitually or extremely late on paying your bills.

The information is tracked by your name, address, and Social Security number. The reporting firms—also called credit bureaus—compile your credit report from the information they receive. Then they sell the report to anyone who provides them with your name, address, and Social Security number and says they want to do business with you. In earlier years, it was mostly lenders who wanted to see your credit report. But now employers, landlords, and insurance companies also want to see your bill-paying behavior before they shake hands on a deal.

The bureaus also sell lists of names of people whose reports meet certain criteria. So, for example, if AARP wants to promote its credit card to people over the age of 50 with good credit reports, it can buy those names and addresses from a credit reporting agency. That's where most of those prescreened offers and dinnertime phone calls originate. In the following chapter, I will tell you exactly how to remove your name from all of those lists, by calling one phone number or using one web site.

But for now, know who these bureaus are and how to find them. You may want to be in touch.

- Equifax
  (800) 685-1111
  www.equifax.com
- Experian
  (888) 397-3742
  www.experian.com
- TransUnion
  (800) 888-4213
  www.transunion.com

Check Your Credit Reports

It may seem threatening enough to know that the credit reporting agencies are compiling massive files about you. What's even more disconcerting is that they are likely to be doing it wrong.

As many as 79 percent of credit reports carry errors, with one in four being serious enough to deny a consumer credit, according to the consumer organization U.S. Public Interest Group. Others have disputed that figure. The credit bureaus, represented by the Consumer Data Industry Association, have said they have removed erroneous data from less than 2 percent of reports. The Government Accountability Office has studied the question and found the answer unknowable.

Whatever the real number is, any mistake on your own credit report is one too many, so you should check to make sure your records are clean. You can do that for free, and it is easy, and there is a right way to do this. Here it is:

Go to this web site: www.annualcreditreport.com.

That is the one official web site set up by all three credit reporting agencies so they can comply with the 2003 law that required them to provide consumers with free copies of their credit reports. Alternatively, you can call (877) 322-8228.

Every year, you are allowed to get one copy of your report for free from each company. Many people just go to this site once a year, click on all three companies, and get their reports. That's a good way to approach it the first time you get your credit reports.

After that, there's a better way to do it: Split them and request a different company's report every four months. So, for example, you can get your Equifax report in February, your Experian report in June, and your TransUnion report in October. You'll effectively be monitoring your profile every four months. If you find a new mistake on one report, then you can go back to the other two agencies and make sure they haven't recorded the same problem.

Should You Always Be Monitoring Your Credit File?

People disagree about how often you need to monitor your credit report. As you will learn in the next chapter, I pay a company to monitor my credit regularly; it gives me peace of mind that nobody is using my name to apply for credit. But if your financial life is stable, if there are no errors on your reports, and if you don't have any immediate plans to apply for a new mortgage or other big loan, taking the three free reports annually could be enough for you.

If you want more than your one free report every year, you can buy additional reports directly from the three credit reporting agencies, Equifax, Experian, and TransUnion.

If you have been the victim of identity theft, or if you are in the process of trying to cleanse errors from your credit file, you might want regular monitoring of your file, at least for a while. Some services that do that are:

- TrueCredit (from TransUnion), www.truecredit.com
- Triple Advantage (from Experian), www.freecreditreport.com
- 3-in-1 Monitoring (from Equifax), www.guardmycredit.com
- Credit Secure (from American Express), www.creditsecure.com

What to Look For

In Figures 3.1, 3.2, and 3.3, I've included three sample credit reports so you have an idea of what they look like. Of course, yours could be longer or shorter, and more or less complicated, depending on your credit history.

Once you get your report, look for the following:

- The basic data is correct: your name, Social Security number, address.
- There's no false information on the report, especially bad false information. If your report says, for example, that you paid your Visa bill late and that's not true, that is bad false information. If it says you have an outstanding bad debt that you know you have paid, that is bad false information.
- There are no sins of omission. Do you have a loan that you have faithfully and responsibly paid on time, but that doesn't show up? It will help your future borrowing power if you get that added to your report.
- Who else is looking at your report? Are there any inquiries on your report that you don't recognize? Lenders who are considering you as a customer will inquire for your credit report. If there are inquiries from lenders you don't know—or haven't applied to recently—this could be a sign that someone else is using your identity. Lenders aren't supposed to access your credit report unless you've submitted an application to them.

Find a Mistake?

Your credit report will include a form for disputing errors. If there are any mistakes in your file, you should start by using this form to request a correction. You should mail the form to the credit bureau at the address listed on the form, and you should use certified mail, so that you have a receipt proving that the credit agency received your form. The credit bureau then has 30 days to check into the error and get back to you. If it doesn't get some verification from the lender or other creditor that the information is correct, it will come off of your report.

Sometimes, the creditor will resubmit the negative report, or will refuse to back down from the initial bad report. (That can happen if

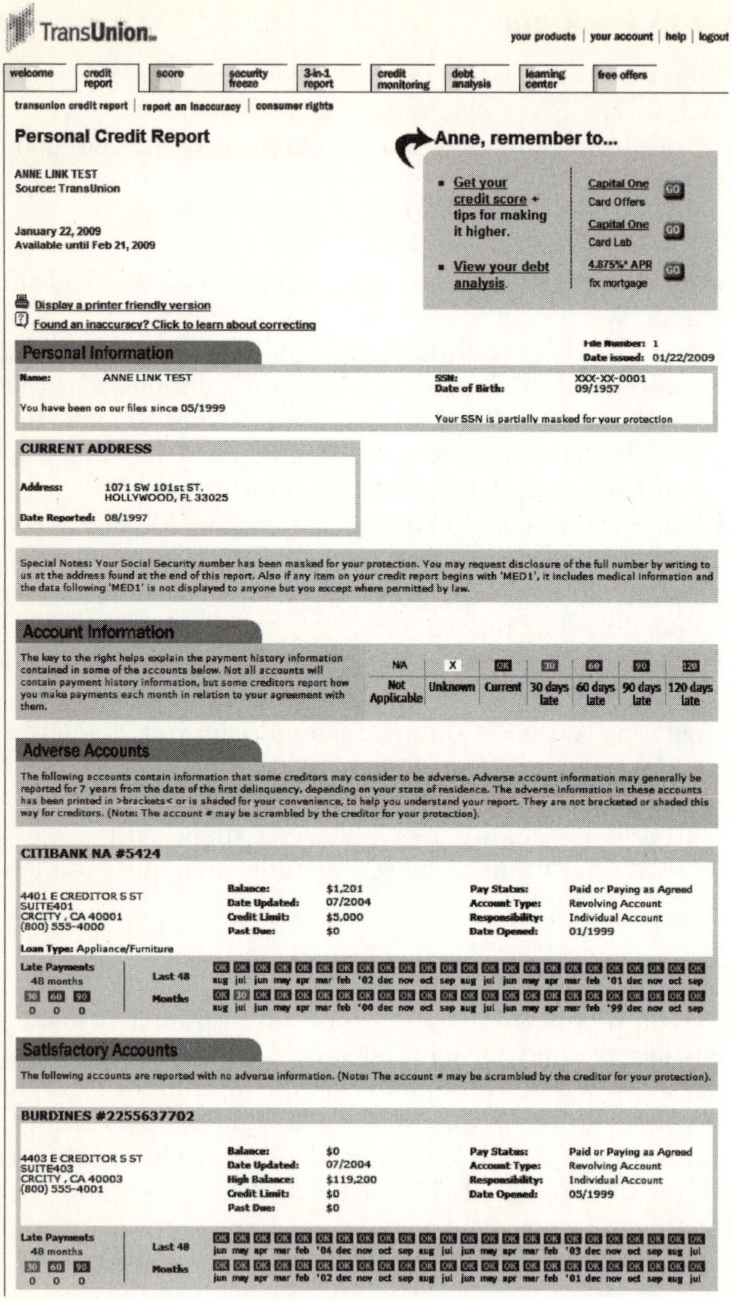

Figure 3.1   TransUnion Sample Credit Report

HRSI BANK #1015905771999

4404 E CREDITOR S ST
SUITE404
CRCITY , CA 40004
(800) 555-4001

Balance:	$0
Date Updated:	07/2004
High Balance:	$119,200
Credit Limit:	$0
Past Due:	$0

Pay Status:	Paid or Paying as Agreed
Account Type:	Revolving Account
Responsibility:	Individual Account
Date Opened:	05/1999

Late Payments
48 months

30	60	90
0	0	0

Last 48 Months

OK OK OK OK OK OK OK OK OK OK OK OK OK OK OK OK OK OK OK OK OK OK OK OK
jun may apr mar feb '04 dec nov oct sep aug jul jun may apr mar feb '03 dec nov oct sep aug jul
OK OK OK OK OK OK OK OK OK OK OK OK OK OK OK OK OK OK OK OK OK OK OK OK
jun may apr mar feb '02 dec nov oct sep aug jul jun may apr mar feb '01 dec nov oct sep aug jul

HRSI BANK-WHIRL #15905771999

4405 E CREDITOR S ST
SUITE405
CRCITY , CA 40005
(800) 555-4001

Balance:	$0
Date Updated:	07/2004
High Balance:	$119,200
Credit Limit:	$0
Past Due:	$0

Pay Status:	Paid or Paying as Agreed
Account Type:	Revolving Account
Responsibility:	Individual Account
Date Opened:	05/1999

Late Payments
48 months

30	60	90
0	0	0

Last 48 Months

OK OK OK OK OK OK OK OK OK OK OK OK OK OK OK OK OK OK OK OK OK OK OK OK
jun may apr mar feb '04 dec nov oct sep aug jul jun may apr mar feb '03 dec nov oct sep aug jul
OK OK OK OK OK OK OK OK OK OK OK OK OK OK OK OK OK OK OK OK OK OK OK OK
jun may apr mar feb '02 dec nov oct sep aug jul jun may apr mar feb '01 dec nov oct sep aug jul

MERC BK OF ST LOUIS NA #3646106

4402 E CREDITOR S ST
SUITE402
CRCITY , CA 40002
(800) 555-4001

Balance:	$0
Date Updated:	07/2004
High Balance:	$119,200
Credit Limit:	$0
Past Due:	$0

Pay Status:	Paid or Paying as Agreed
Account Type:	Installment Account
Responsibility:	Individual Account
Date Opened:	05/1999

Late Payments
48 months

30	60	90
0	0	0

Last 48 Months

OK OK OK OK OK OK OK OK OK OK OK OK OK OK OK OK OK OK OK OK OK OK OK OK
jun may apr mar feb '04 dec nov oct sep aug jul jun may apr mar feb '03 dec nov oct sep aug jul
OK OK OK OK OK OK OK OK OK OK OK OK OK OK OK OK OK OK OK OK OK OK OK OK
jun may apr mar feb '02 dec nov oct sep aug jul jun may apr mar feb '01 dec nov oct sep aug jul

Regular Inquiries

The following companies have received your credit report. Their inquiries remain on your credit report for two years.

INQUIRY ANALYSIS NAME 1
5501 NW INQUIRY E ST
SUITE 501
INCITY , CA 50001
Phone number not available

Requested On: 10/07/2004
Inquiry Type: Individual

Permissible Purpose: abc efgh jklmnopqrst vwxy a cd fghijk mnopqrs

Inquiry Analysis

The companies listed in the regular inquiry section of your report that received your file in the last 90 days provided the following input on their request.

INQUIRY ANALYSIS NAME 1

Requested On: 10/07/2004

Identifying information they provided:
ANNIE LINK TEST

1101 CURRENT ST.
PERCITY, CA 10001

Should you wish to contact TransUnion, you may do so,

Report an Inaccuracy:
To learn about reporting an inaccuracy click here.

By Mail:
TransUnion Consumer Relations
PO Box 2000
Chester, PA 19022-2000

By Phone:
(800) 916-8800
Our business hours in your time zone are 8:30 a.m. to 4:30 p.m., Monday through Friday, except major holidays. Please have your TransUnion file number available (located at the top of this report).

Figure 3.1   (Continued)

∷ Experian
A world of insight

Online Personal Credit Report from Experian for

Experian credit report prepared for
JOHN Q CONSUMER
Your report number is
1562064065 [1]
Report date:
04/24/2007

Index:
- Potentially negative items
- Accounts in good standing
- Requests for your credit history
- Personal information
- Important message from Experian [2]
- Contact us

Report number:

You will need your report number to contact Experian online, by phone or by mail.

Index:

Navigate through the sections of your credit report using these links.

Experian collects and organizes information about you and your credit history from public records, your creditors and other reliable sources. Experian makes your credit history available to your current and prospective creditors, employers and others as allowed by law, which can expedite your ability to obtain credit and can make offers of credit available to you. We do not grant or deny credit; each credit grantor makes that decision based on its own guidelines.

To return to your report in the near future, log on to www...experian.com/consumer and select "View your report again" or "Dispute" and then enter your report number.

If you disagree with information in this report, return to the Report Summary page and follow the instructions for disputing.

Potentially Negative Items [3]   back to top

Public Records

Credit grantors may carefully review the items listed below when they check your credit history. Please note that the account information connected with some public records, such as bankruptcy, also may appear with your credit items listed later in this report.

MAIN COUNTY CLERK

Address: 123 MAINTOWN S BUFFALO , NY 10000	Identification Number: 1	Plaintiff: ANY COMMISSIONER O.
Status: Civil claim paid.		Status Details: This item was verified and updated in Apr 2007.

Date Filed: 10/15/2006	Claim Amount: $200
Date Resolved: 03/04/2007	Liability Amount: NA
Responsibility: INDIVIDUAL	

Potentially negative items:

Items that creditors may view less favorably. It includes the creditor's name and address, your account number (shortened for security), account status, type and terms of the account and any other information reported to Experian by the creditor. Also includes any bankruptcy, lien and judgment information obtained directly from the courts.

Status:

Indicates the current status of the account.

Credit Items

For your protection, the last few digits of your account numbers do not display.

ABCD BANKS

Address: 100 CENTER RD BUFFALO, NY 10000 (555) 555-5555	Account Number: 1000000....
Status: Paid/Past due 60 days. [4]	

Date Opened: 10/2005	Type: Installment	Credit Limit/Original Amount: $523
Reported Since: 11/2005	Terms: 12 Months	High Balance: NA
Date of Status: 04/2007	Monthly Payment: $0	Recent Balance: $0 as of 04/2007 Recent Payment: $0
Last Reported: 04/2007	Responsibility: Individual	

Account History:
60 days as of 12-2006
30 days as of 11-2006

If you believe information in your report is inaccurate, you can dispute that item quickly, effectively and cost free by using Experian's online dispute service located at:

www.experian.com/disputes

Disputing online is the fastest way to address any concern you may have about the information in your credit report.

Figure 3.2   Experian Sample Credit Report

MAIN COLL AGENCIES

Address:	Account Number:	Original Creditor:
PO BOX 123	0123456789	TELEVISE CABLE COMM.
ANYTOWN, PA 10000		
(555) 555-5555		

Status: Collection account. $95 past due as of 4-2000.

Date Opened:	Type:	Credit Limit/Original Amount:
01/2005	Installment	$95
Reported Since:	Terms:	High Balance:
04/2005	NA	NA
Date of Status:	Monthly	Recent Balance:
04/2005	Payment:	$95 as of 04/2005
	$0	Recent Payment:
Last Reported:	Responsibility:	$0
04/2005	Individual	

Your statement: ITEM DISPUTED BY CONSUMER

Accounts in good standing:

Lists accounts that have a positive status and may be viewed favorably by creditors. Some creditors do not report to us, so some of your accounts may not be listed.

Account History:
Collection as of 4-2005

Accounts in Good Standing   **5**   back to top

AUTOMOBILE AUTO FINANCE

Address:	Account Number:
100 MAIN ST E	12345678996....
SMALLTOWN, MD 90001	
(555) 555-5555	

Status: Open/Never late.

Type:

Account type indicates whether your account is a revolving or an installment account.

Date Opened:	Type: **6**	Credit Limit/Original Amount:
01/2006	Installment	$10,355
Reported Since:	Terms:	High Balance:
01/2006	65 Months	NA
Date of Status:	Monthly	Recent Balance:
04/2007	Payment:	$7,984 as of 04/2007
	$210	Recent Payment:
Last Reported:	Responsibility:	$0
04/2007	Individual	

MAIN

Address:	Account Number:
PO BOX 1234	1234567899876
FORT LAUDERDALE, FL 10009	

Status: Closed/Never late.

Date Opened:	Type:	Credit Limit/Original Amount:
03/1997	Revolving	NA
Reported Since:	Terms:	High Balance:
03/1997	1 Months	$3,228
Date of Status:	Monthly	Recent Balance:
08/2006	Payment:	$0 /paid as of 08/2006
	$0	Recent Payment:
Last Reported:	Responsibility:	$0
08/2006	Individual	

Your statement:
Account closed at consumer's request

Figure 3.2   (Continued)

34   Master Your Debt

Requests for Your Credit History   **7**   back to top

Requests Viewed By Others

We make your credit history available to your current and prospective creditors and employers as allowed by law. Personal data about you may be made available to companies whose products and services may interest you.

The section below lists all who have requested in the recent past to review your credit history as a result of actions involving you, such as the completion of a credit application or the transfer of an account to a collection agency, application for insurance, mortgage or loan application, etc. Creditors may view these requests when evaluating your creditworthiness.

HOMESALE REALTY CO

Address:	Date of Request:
2000 S MAINROAD BLVD STE ANYTOWN CA 11111 (555) 555-5555	07/16/2006

Comments:
Real estate loan on behalf of 3903 MERCHANTS EXPRESS M. This inquiry is scheduled to continue on record until 8-2008.

M & T BANK

Address:	Date of Request:
PO BOX 100 BUFFALO NY 10000 (555) 555-5555	02/23/2006

Comments:
Permissible purpose. This inquiry is scheduled to continue on record until 3-2008.

WESTERN FUNDING INC

Address:	Date of Request:
191 W MAIN AVE STE 100 INTOWN CA 10000 (559) 555-5555	01/25/2006

Comments:
Permissible purpose. This inquiry is scheduled to continue on record until 2-2008.

Requests Viewed Only By You

The section below lists all who have a permissible purpose by law and have requested in the recent past to review your information. You may not have initiated these requests, so you may not recognize each source. We offer information about you to those with a permissible purpose, for example, to:

- other creditors who want to offer you preapproved credit;
- an employer who wishes to extend an offer of employment;
- a potential investor in assessing the risk of a current obligation;
- Experian or other credit reporting agencies to process a report for you;
- your existing creditors to monitor your credit activity (date listed may reflect only the most recent request).

We report these requests **only to you** as a record of activities. We **do not** provide this information to other creditors who evaluate your creditworthiness.

MAIN BANK USA

Address:	Date of Request:
1 MAIN CTR AA 11 BUFFALO NY 14203	08/10/2006

MYTOWN BANK

Address:	Date of Request:
PO BOX 825 MYTOWN DE 10000 (555) 555-5555	08/05/2006

INTOWN DATA CORPS

Address:	Date of Request:
2000 S MAINTOWN BLVD STE INTOWN CO 11111 (555) 555-5555	07/16/2006

Requests for your credit history:

Also called "inquiries," requests for your credit history are logged on your report whenever anyone reviews your credit information. There are two types of inquiries.

i.
Inquiries resulting from a transaction initiated by you. These include inquiries from your applications for credit, insurance, housing or other loans. They also include transfer of an account to a collection agency. Creditors may view these items when evaluating your creditworthiness.

ii.
Inquiries resulting from transactions you may not have initiated but that are allowed under the FCRA. These include preapproved offers, as well as for employment, investment review, account monitoring by existing creditors, and requests by you for your own report. These items are shown only to you and have no impact on your creditworthiness or risk scores.

Figure 3.2   (Continued)

Personal Information   **8**

The following information is reported to us by you, your creditors and other sources. Each source may report your personal information differently, which may result in variations of your name, address, Social Security number, etc. As part of our fraud prevention efforts, a notice with additional information may appear. As a security precaution, the Social Security number that you used to obtain this report is not displayed. The Name identification number and Address identification number are how our system identifies variations of your name and address that may appear on your report. The Geographical Code shown with each address identifies the state, county, census tract, block group and Metropolitan Statistical Area associated with each address.

Personal information:

Personal information associated with your history that has been reported to Experian by you, your creditors and other sources.

Names:
JOHN Q CONSUMER
Name identification number: 15621

JONATHON Q CONSUMER
Name identification number: 15622

J Q CONSUMER
Name identification number: 15623

Social Security number variations:
999999999

Year of birth:
1959

Spouse or co-applicant:
JANE

Employers:
ABCDE ENGINEERING CORP

Telephone numbers:
(555) 555 5555 Residential

Address: 123 MAIN STREET
ANYTOWN, MD 90001-9999
Address identification number:
0277741504
Type of Residence: Multifamily
Geographical Code: 0-156510-31-8840   **9**

Address: 555 SIMPLE PLACE
ANYTOWN, MD 90002-7777
Address identification number:
0170088050
Type of Residence: Single family
Geographical Code: 0-176510-33-8840

Address: 999 HIGH DRIVE APT 15B
ANYTOWN, MD 90003-5555
Address identification number:
0170129301
Type of Residence: Apartment complex
Geographical Code: 0-156510-31-8840

May include name and Social Security number variations, employers, telephone numbers, etc. Experian lists all variations so you know what is being reported to us as belonging to you.

Address information:
Your current address and previous address(es)

Personal statement:
Any personal statement that you added to your report appears here.

Your Personal Statement   **10**

No general personal statements appear on your report.

Important Message From Experian   back to top

By law, we cannot disclose certain medical information (relating to physical, mental, or behavioral health or condition). Although we do not generally collect such information, it could appear in the name of a data furnisher (i.e., "Cancer Center") that reports your payment history to us. If so, those names display in your report, but in reports to others they display only as MEDICAL PAYMENT DATA. Consumer statements included on your report at your request that contain medical information are disclosed to others.

Note - statements remain as part of the report for two years and display to anyone who has permission to review your report.

Contacting Us   back to top

Contact address and phone number for your area will display here.

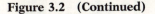

Figure 3.2   (Continued)

there was a dispute over a bill that was unresolved.) You don't have much recourse in that case, other than negotiating directly with the creditor. You should try, because many lenders and others will want to keep existing customers happy. But you may not prevail. You can also put a note into your file, explaining the dispute, but that will not help you much. Notes aren't carried forward into scores, and that is where most lending decisions are made.

Find Bad Reports That Aren't Mistakes?

You may have some black marks on your credit file that you earned, fair and square, by paying bills late or not at all. You can't erase them, and you shouldn't trust any credit repair company that promises to clean your credit report for a fee.

Equifax Credit Report
Online Sample

1. **Equifax Credit Report:** your complete credit history from Equifax

2. **Account Information:** a complete list of all credit accounts and their status at the time the information was reported by your lenders and creditors

3. **Inquiries:** companies that have requested your credit file for marketing purposes (as permitted by law), for a periodic review of your credit, and/or to consider extending credit or granting a loan

4. **Negative Information:** accounts that contain a negative status

  • **Collections:** accounts that your lenders and/or creditors have turned over to a collection agency

  • **Public Records:** includes items obtained from local, state and federal courts, such as bankruptcies, liens and judgments

5. **Personal Information:** identification information including your name, Social Security Number, date of birth, address information and employment information

6. **Dispute File Information:** how to dispute information found on your credit report

7. **Print Credit Report:** print out your complete Equifax Credit Report for future reference

Figure 3.3   Equifax Sample Credit Report

But, like any other historical record, it becomes less painful as it recedes into the past. Credit scores count new records more heavily than old ones; even if a late payment remains in your file, it won't hurt your borrowing power as much if it was four years ago than if it was placed there last Tuesday.

Furthermore, even the worst black marks—default and bankruptcy—eventually come off. Bad information can stay on your report for seven years; some bankruptcies can stay in for 10. Eventually, it will disappear, and if you've lived on the straight and narrow for seven years, you'll have a clean credit report.

If you have recently gone through a difficult time and paid several bills late, you can contact your lenders and ask them to withdraw a negative report. Sometimes they will, especially now when many good customers have fallen behind in the recession. They may be more concerned about keeping you as a satisfied customer than letting that one report stand, or they may be persuaded by your story that the late payments were an anomaly.

One new company, called SmartCredit (www.smartcredit.com), claims to have push-button online access to most major lenders; sign up for its service, at $20 a month or more, and you can dispute negative information in your credit file by clicking on it at its web site. This may be especially useful for people who have been late on their payments but want to ask creditors for goodwill adjustments to their reports. But I'm not sure that many merchants would be inclined to make goodwill corrections at the push of a button; and it's a rather pricey service. You could put in the time and contact creditors directly instead. Another reputable service called Credit Report ABC that helps you dispute and remove derogatory information from your credit report can be found at www.creditreportabc.com.

It's Your Score That Really Counts

Making your credit file as pristine as possible is important, because it is the data in the file that will be used to produce your credit score, and *that* is the number that can make or break your financial future. People with good credit scores get the best deals: They buy cars on zero percent credit cards, lock in mortgages at below-market rates, and skim the best preapproved offers in the marketplace. A good credit score is worth more than $1 million, according to estimates published at TheStreet.com, a personal finance and investing web site. "Your credit score is your currency," says Ken Lin of Credit Karma, a Web-based company that distributes information about credit scores. "You can leverage it to get advantage in a financial transaction."

Those with low credit scores, meanwhile, are dumped into subprime world: a scary place of double-digit mortgages, 19 percent car loans, extra fees, unscrupulous operators, and no credit when you need it.

You can raise your score, and there are some very specific strategies for doing that, even on a short-term basis. But first you have to understand where scoring comes from.

Mathematicians were messing around with consumer scoring for decades. The idea that an algorithm could be used to grade a customer's creditworthiness had broad appeal to companies that were looking for a quick way to qualify and disqualify customers. In the mid-1980s, the company then named Fair Isaac Corporation (and now named FICO) created credit scores based on the data in credit reports. Mortgage lenders, in particular, loved the scores; they could use them to set mortgage rates that matched the profiles of particular customers.

When financial professionals talk about credit scores, they are almost always talking about this FICO score, which is the most widely used credit score there is. But now, many other companies have started publishing their own scores. Each of the big three credit reporting agencies has its own scoring formula, and all three banded together to create one joint scoring formula, called the VantageScore. There are other third-party scorers, too: Some of the credit monitoring web sites, like SmartScore.com, create their own proprietary scoring models. In addition, the various scoring companies also fine-tune their scores to better fit different lenders and merchants that might want the scores. For example, there are auto scores that are calculated differently than mortgage scores, but based on the same data.

How to See Your Scores

The most important score, because it remains the most widely used score, is the FICO score. You actually have three FICO scores—one based on data from each of the big three credit bureaus. So you have an Equifax FICO score, an Experian FICO score, and a TransUnion FICO score. Lenders can buy and use all three of these, but as this book goes to press, you have access to only two of them: You can buy your Equifax FICO and your TransUnion FICO at the myFICO web site (www.myfico.com), but Experian has decided to limit access to the Experian FICO scores for now. You can't get these scores for free, as every time some lender or publisher has tried to give consumers access to their scores, FICO has shut them down. The scoring formulas are proprietary, cost a fortune to develop, and are worth a fortune to protect, so FICO is trying its hardest to hold on to its competitive advantage. The three credit bureaus all sell their own scores, too.

But other scorekeepers are building their models so that their scoring systems look like and correlate with FICO scores, and you can sometimes get those for free. Internet company Credit Karma (www.creditkarma.com) offers TransUnion scores for free. But be careful. There are numerous sites that promise free credit reports and free credit scores, but they are rarely really free. They typically offer various subscription and monitoring services that can get costly, and that come with the free scores.

Even though some consumers have gotten obsessed with monitoring their scores and making sure they are as high as can be, you don't really have to monitor your credit score as much as you monitor the accuracy of your credit report. You should, however, get your scores at least a year before you intend to borrow big money with a new mortgage or car loan, and keep checking them every month or so as you approach that loan application. That gives you time to improve your grade if your score isn't where you'd like it to be.

Do You Have a Good Grade?

The FICO score is based on a scale of 300 to 850, and the higher your score is, the better. The median score in the United States is 723. There was a time, before the recent credit crunch, when anything over a 650 would get you any loan you wanted. Now, with lenders tightening credit and trying to improve the quality of their loan portfolios, they are looking for ever-higher scores. A top-tier score now is above 760, says Craig Watts of FICO. And you'd better believe that that makes a huge difference. Look at this chart, from FICO. It shows the impact of the FICO score on the interest rates and monthly payments on a 30-year fixed-rate mortgage.

FICO Score	Interest Rate	Monthly Payment
760–850	4.555%	$1,530
700–759	4.777%	$1,570
680–699	4.954%	$1,602
660–679	5.168%	$1,641
640–659	5.598%	$1,722
620–639	6.144%	$1,827

The borrower with a middling 650 score would pay $69,120 more over the life of the loan than the consumer with a score above 760.

And for a car loan? Here's how different scores would affect the rates and payments on a three-year $25,000 car loan.

FICO Score	Interest Rate	Monthly Payment
720–850	5.961%	$760
690–719	7.445%	$777
660–689	8.843%	$793
620–659	11.655%	$826
590–619	15.440%	$872
500–589	16.153%	$881

That under-589 subprime borrower will pay $4,356 more for his car than the top scorer will.

You Can Improve Your Credit Score

Credit scores are dynamic—they are changing constantly based on changes in your credit file. You can have a different credit score at the beginning of the month, when you have big balances on your credit cards, than you do at the end of the month.

There are techniques that you can use to improve your credit score, and some of them work very fast, within months. Other changes take longer, but not as long as you might think. Let's take Robert, a guy who admits to "bad behavior out of college" involving credit cards. He ended up defaulting on some of his credit card debt, and there were mistakes in his credit file, too. "In 2004, my score was barely above 500," he remembers. But he wised up. He set about paying down his debts, paying off old debts, and applying judiciously for new credit cards but barely using them. He spent a lot of time trolling on the discussion groups at the myFICO web site, where consumers trade credit score strategies. And now his score is over 800, and he spends more time fielding great financial offers than he does hiding from debt collectors.

You, too, can improve your credit score, but first you have to know how your credit score is built. Of course, the secret algorithm *is* a secret. But FICO has released some solid information about the components of the scoring formula that can give us insights into how to move those scores. Here's what goes into the secret formula, and how you can use this information to improve your score.

- **Your payment history.** This is the most important component of the score, making up 35 percent of it. If you have a long history of paying your bills on time, that will give you a higher score. Typically, your payment history on debts such as credit cards is the biggest part of this component. But if you are habitually late on other bills, such as your phone or cable bill, those creditors can also put that information on your credit report and it could feed into your credit score.

  How to use this to improve your score: Start paying your bills on time, even if you have mistakes in your past. If certain debts that you have been paying don't appear on your credit report, call the creditors and ask them to submit your records to the credit bureaus. If you have bad debts or late payments in your background, you can call creditors and ask them to remove them from your file, or you can just wait for the day when they come off. As they recede into the past, they will become less important to your score.

- **The amount you owe.** This makes up 30 percent of your score. The formula looks at your credit utilization—how much of your available credit are you using? If you're maxing out on any of your credit cards, this can hurt you. It can also hurt you if you owe money on lots of different cards and loans.

  How to use this to improve your score: Find money to pay down your debts so that you aren't maxing out on any cards. Call your credit card company and ask for an increase in your credit line. (Note that in the past year some banks have gone the other way, and have cut unused credit lines, hurting consumer scores.) If you owe money on several different credit cards, try to pay most of them off, so that you're carrying a balance on only one or two. But don't go so far that you max out that card. If you're trying to raise your score in advance of a mortgage loan, you might even pull money out of savings to pay down your debts.

- **The length of your credit history.** The scorekeepers like to see old accounts and a long history of maintaining those accounts in a timely way. This makes up 15 percent of your score.

   How to use this to improve your score: If you stop using an old credit card because you no longer like its rate or benefits, don't cancel it; just put it away in a drawer and keep the account open. Use it infrequently for a minor charge, every six months or so, so that it will stay active, and then pay it off promptly.

- **New credit.** Have you been applying for a lot of new credit? What proportion of your total credit consists of new loans and cards? That can push down your score. This makes up 10 percent of your score.

   How to use this to improve your score: If you apply for a lot of loans at once, it can look as if you're scrambling for money and in trouble, so don't do that. But the FICO folks understand that if you're looking for one new mortgage or car loan, you might have to make a few inquiries to choose the right one for you. So making multiple inquiries for the same kind of loan doesn't hurt your score, if you do them all within a short time frame—a month or so. If you think you want a new credit card, apply for it a year or more before you are going to apply for a mortgage. Don't apply for credit cards within weeks of looking for a car or home loan.

- **The type of credit.** It's good for your score to have a mix of kinds of credit. A large, fixed-rate loan, such as a student loan, coupled with a couple of credit cards and an installment loan will result in a better score than if you've had only one credit card or one student loan—assuming, of course, that you're paying your bills on time.

   How to use this to improve your score: Over time, give yourself experience with different kinds of credit. Instead of putting your new computer on your credit card, for example, you might get a loan from the computer store and pay it off over time.

What's Not in Your Score

Your score isn't the only thing that determines whether you get a loan. Your income counts, too. A newly unemployed person with a high score may still be turned down for a loan. The score doesn't reflect anything about your employment situation. And there are other issues that aren't reflected in the score, either. Your score doesn't include information about the interest rates on your current loans, or other obligations, like child support or alimony. It also doesn't include information on whether you are participating in a credit counseling program, though of course if that program is the result of (or results in) your not paying your bills in full and in a timely manner, *that* will be in your score.

What If . . . ?

If you're a year—or even six months—away from applying for a loan, it's a good idea to fine-tune your credit score. There are several different score simulators online that will let you see how different actions can change your score. Try these, and see what you learn:

- Bankrate: www.bankrate.com/brm/fico/calc.asp
- Credit Karma: www.creditkarma.com/simulator
- FICO: www.myfico.com (When you buy your score here, you get access to the score simulator.)

Credit scores are not going to go away. If anything, they will become more and more important as banks and other lenders try to improve their lending practices as they emerge from recession. You'll get better offers and save hundreds, thousands, and perhaps hundreds of thousands of dollars over your lifetime of borrowing if you play the game along with them.

4

Avoiding a Modern-Day Identity Crisis

If you think you won't be the victim of identity theft because you're just an average person with an unimpressive bank account, think again. You aren't immune, even if you use a shredder for your monthly bills, are pretty careful with your credit cards, and avoid online banking. Even if your bank asks for an ID every time you try to cash a check—and you've been going there for years, waiting for the teller to recognize you—you're not protected from identity theft.

Anyone who thinks that identity theft can't happen to them is "alarmingly disconnected" from reality, as John Sileo, author of *Stolen Lives: Identity Theft Prevention Made Simple* (DaVinci Publishing, 2005)—one of the best books on this subject—likes to say. Every time I give a speech I ask the audience if anyone's ever had their identity stolen, and invariably some hands go in the air. Identity theft can happen to anyone, at any time, and it could take days, weeks, or even years to discover it—and longer to clean it up. It can create a huge mess, and it can happen to you.

Identity theft occurs when someone acquires a piece of your personal information and uses it to commit fraud. In its extreme form, a thief with your Social Security number could be out there living an alternative version of your life: opening bank accounts; stocking up on houses, jewelry, and cars; traveling around the world; dealing drugs or carrying out other crimes; and telling everyone he or she is you. More typical is the version of ID theft that occurs when someone gets hold of your credit card number and then goes on a one-day shopping spree until you (or your card issuer) catch the problem and cancel the card. In even its mildest version, identity theft can really hurt, and I'm not just talking about the psychological pain of being a victim: It can trash your credit report, and that can take a long, long time to fix.

Identity theft is burgeoning. In 2008, the number of instances of identity fraud rose 22 percent to near-record levels, with one of every 23 adult Americans being victimized, according to Javelin Strategy & Research, a financial services consulting firm. Some $48 billion was lost. You may think that identity theft is a growing phenomenon because of the growth of Internet shopping and banking—that all of those bits of data flying around the Web lead inevitably to more theft. And there are certainly high-tech frauds to worry about. But the most common form of ID theft still occurs by old-fashioned methods: A pickpocket grabs your wallet; a dishonest restaurant employee pulls your credit card number off the slip in the trash.

If you want to know everything about how identity theft occurs, I recommend that you go further than this chapter—buy John Sileo's book. His motto is "Think like a spy" (his informative web site is at www.thinklikeaspy.com), and he offers checklists and action plans for people who want to do everything in their power to protect their financial and personal information.

He also tells some strange and distressing stories about ID theft victims. In California, apparently, it's not unusual for women to use other women's names and credit cards when getting breast augmentation, tummy tucks, and other plastic surgeries. Victims have not only lost their credit cards; they've been subject to follow-up phone calls from surgeons about how their breasts are doing and had to worry about proving that their body parts were their own or making sure their medical records were accurate.

So yes, ID theft can get pretty bizarre. But there are ways for you to protect yourself from identity theft. All of those methods I mentioned at the beginning of this chapter—shredding bills, being careful about your credit cards—help. But they aren't enough. There are other steps you can and should take to make sure your financial identity and the dollars in your bank account remain in your control.

Learn the Basics

If you know how identity thieves operate, you'll have a better chance of cutting them off at the pass. Here are the many ways that the Federal Trade Commission says identity thieves can get hold of your information.

- **Stealing.** They steal credit card bills and convenience checks out of mailboxes. They steal wallets and purses wherever they find them.
- **Diverting.** They file a change of address form for *you* with the post office; your bills and statements get diverted to their address.
- **Dumpster diving.** They pull credit card slips out of restaurant trash bins and bank statements out of the recycle bin in the front of your house.
- **Shoulder surfing.** They stand next to you at the ATM or checkout machine and read your personal identification number (PIN) as you key it in.
- **Pretending to be trustworthy.** Sadly, the most costly identity thefts are usually carried out by people that the victims know. A dishonest "friend," relative, neighbor, or household employee can just copy the important numbers they find sitting out on your desk.

Then there are the new-tech ways to steal identities.

- **Skimming.** They put a special storage device on a store's card processing equipment or an ATM and collect all the numbers that go through it.
- **Phishing.** They pretend to be your bank (or eBay) sending you an important account update via e-mail. You click on the link to verify your information, and instead you'll have clicked through to a fake site that looks like your bank's site but exists to grab personal financial information.
- **Fake networking.** They set up Wi-Fi networks in public spots, like parks or airports, to collect information about you when you go on what you think is a safe network to check your bank balance.

- **Hacking.** They put spyware on your computer that sends them messages with your passwords and account numbers.

Then What?

Once an unscrupulous person has your Social Security number or your bank account number and PIN, the thief can really go to town. Here are some of the kinds of things an identity thief can (and will) do with that information.

- Open new credit card accounts in your name, with a different address. You'll never see the bills, but the delinquencies will show up on your credit report.
- Start new utility services for phone, wireless, cable TV, electricity, or gas. Again, you won't see the bills, but the bad debts will follow you around.
- Create counterfeit checks using your name and account number. By the time you get your monthly statement, your money may be gone and your mortgage check will have bounced.
- Claim government benefits using your Social Security number; get a driver's license or other ID with the thief's picture and your name.
- File a fraudulent tax return from "you" and get a refund.
- Live as you. Get a job, rent a house, have surgery, drive drunk, or get arrested under your name.

Prevention Is Easier Than Cleaning Up Later

It is possible to recover from even the worst identity theft, but it's a huge nightmare that you would be better off not dealing with. Make it harder for thieves to pick on you by protecting your financial information. Here are some good habits to adopt.

- Carry around fewer bits of info in your wallet. Leave your Social Security card at home (or, even better, in your safe-deposit box). Don't go shopping with all of your credit cards.
- Keep your checks clean. Don't print your Social Security number or driver's license number on your checks. In fact, you are better off not keeping your checkbook in your purse at all.

- Try to get your Social Security number removed from IDs like your health insurance card or your driver's license. Some states and insurance companies will allow you to use an alternative ID number.
- Only use credit cards that carry your photo ID on them.
- Copy your wallet. This won't prevent identity theft, but it will make recovery a lot easier. Go to your local copy shop, empty your wallet onto one of the machines, and make a copy of every card. Turn them over and copy the backs. Keep a copy filed safely away at home or in your safe-deposit box.
- Buy a shredder and use it for any bills, checks, statements, or other documents that have your personal information on them, including preapproved credit card offers.
- Protect your phone and your computer with a password.
- Use a locking file cabinet and a safe-deposit box for important papers.
- Keep up-to-date antivirus and antispyware on your computer.
- Use different passwords for different Internet sites. Change the passwords on your bank and brokerage sites regularly. Keep a record of your passwords on a piece of paper, but keep that piece of paper locked up in your file cabinet or safe-deposit box.
- Receive and pay bills online whenever possible—done correctly, this is more secure than your mailbox!
- Monitor your credit reports on a regular basis, as I described in Chapter 3.

Opt Out

The fewer mailing lists you are on, the less your information is circulated, sold, and resold. And by opting out of most offers, you'll also cut down on the nuisance of junk mail, spam, and dinner-hour phone calls. Here is how to opt out of most unwanted offers.

- Tell your bank to discontinue sending convenience checks or other card promotions about your account.
- Stop prescreened credit offers by calling 1-888-5OPTOUT (1-888-567-8688) or by registering at www.optoutprescreen.com.
- Stop annoying telemarketing calls by putting your name on the national Do Not Call Registry at www.donotcall.gov. You can also

(Continued)

contact your state consumer affairs office to see if there is an additional Do Not Call list there.

- Reduce junk mail, ironically, by registering at the web site of the industry trade group, the Direct Marketing Association (www.dma consumers.org).
- Remove your name and other identifying information from online directories, such as Google's reverse phone directory, as you find it. This will make it harder for your high school friends to find you, but will also keep you off a number of marketing lists.
- Opt out on a case-by-case basis. Just about every institution or business you deal with will send you some sort of privacy statement, notifying you that your information will be shared with partner businesses. They usually include procedures for opting out of that list sharing.
- Just say no to special offers. Often, when you register on web sites or buy items online, you'll find a (usually prechecked) box that says, "Please tell me about special discounts and offers that are great for me!" or some such. Uncheck the box before you finish the transaction.

About Fraud Alerts and Credit Freezes

The best way to prevent someone else from using your good name to apply for credit is to control your credit reports. There are two ways to do that: You can flag your credit files with fraud alerts, or you can freeze your credit files altogether.

I'll explain all about these techniques here, but first I'll let you in on one secret: The credit reporting agencies don't like fraud alerts and freezes. That's because they make their money selling your files to would-be creditors. The harder it is for them to hand out those files, the less money they can make selling them. The credit reporting bureaus have made it easier for consumers to place fraud alerts and freezes on their accounts only because they were forced into that position through state laws, lawsuits, and the threat of federal legislation.

Consumer groups, by contrast, love these tactics. Consumer Action, a national advocacy organization that focuses on credit issues, recommends that consumers who aren't expecting to apply for any new credit freeze their files.

The credit reporting agencies don't like you to know this, but you can place a fraud alert in your credit files, even if you have no specific reason to suspect that you've been a victim. To place a fraud alert in your credit files, you must notify one of these three agencies:

- Equifax: 1-800-525-6285; www.equifax.com
- Experian: 1-888-397-3742; www.experian.com
- TransUnion: 1-800-680-7289; www.transunion.com

Whichever agency you notify will notify the other two, and all three will flag your credit reports for 90 days. That means that whenever potential creditors request your files, they will be notified that you may be a victim of identity theft. The creditors will most likely respond to that notification by contacting you directly before they approve any credit applications.

The three agencies look at these fraud alerts as a way to manage accounts in which there is reason to believe information may have been compromised. But consumer groups—and I agree with them— see them as a permanent way to keep tighter controls on your credit report. If you want to keep alerts on your credit files all the time, you will have to renew your request every three months. (If you've actually been a victim of identity theft, your account can be flagged for seven years. Read more about how to recover from identity theft in Chapter 10.)

Actually *freezing* your credit file is a whole other level of control. It means nobody—not even creditors you want to borrow from—will be able to access your credit report. You will have to let all three agencies know you want your files frozen and you may have to pay $10 to each one to accomplish that, depending on what state you live in. Once your account is frozen, you can "defrost" it—lift the freeze—by notifying the agency that you want to do that. If you rarely apply for new credit and don't expect to do that anytime soon, then you should consider freezing your files. My identity theft mentor, John Sileo, thinks the freezing tactic is a good idea. "Had I frozen my credit neither of my cases of identity theft would have happened," he said, noting that he was ripped off once by a stranger who bought a house in his name, and once by a business partner who committed fraud in his name.

If you do freeze your account, lift the freeze four to six months before you expect to borrow money, so that you have time to make sure your records are in order before you apply for that car loan, credit card, or mortgage.

And now I will tell you what I do, personally, with all of this. I pay a company called Lifelock (www.lifelock.com/moneyanswers, 800-LIFELOCK, mention promo code Moneyanswers to qualify for a discount) to guard my credit report for me. For $110 a year, Lifelock keeps renewing fraud alerts on my credit files, so I don't have to remember to keep doing it myself. The company also does things like monitor address databases and hacker web sites to make sure my address doesn't get changed (a sign that someone is trying to hijack my credit card statements) and my personal data doesn't show up. Other companies that provide similar services are Identity Guard (www.identityguard.com) and TrustedID (www.trustedid.com).

Of course, I could do much of this myself, but I don't want to take the time. Some critics have suggested that the actual risk of being badly victimized by new account fraud actually is pretty low, much lower than Lifelock and these other companies would have you believe. Javelin Strategy & Research has found its incidence declining to around 1 percent of the population. So why do I keep signing up with Lifelock? I think it is a good idea because the cost of doing so is small but the potential damage of being hit by ID theft is so enormous that a person should do everything possible to prevent getting hit.

You May Already Be a Victim

How will you even know if your identity has been stolen? You might get strange phone calls from bill collectors for debts you don't even have. Or you'll be unable to get a new credit card or car loan, even though you are pretty sure you should qualify. Perhaps you don't get your credit card bill on time. Or you find unauthorized charges on your credit card or bank withdrawals you didn't make. Your credit card issuer might call you to ask about unusual behavior on the card.

If you suspect you have been victimized by identity theft, the first step is to notify all three credit bureaus, your bank, and all of your creditors, and let them know you suspect something is amiss. Get copies of your statements and your files, so you can see if there are other problems.

The Federal Trade Commission (FTC) has an excellent web site with information and help for people who have become ID theft victims at www.ftc.gov/bcp/edu/microsites/idtheft/. There you can file a complaint with the FTC, and also find the FTC's ID Theft Affidavit form. You should fill that out and use it to demonstrate to creditors, credit reporting agencies, and others that you have been victimized in this way. You can also use it to close any accounts that have been issued in your name. You should also notify the police. While it's unlikely they'll put a lot of manpower into finding the person who used your good name, having the police report will help you to straighten out your accounts and reports. It will help you get your credit reports cleansed of problematic accounts opened by others.

Many identity thefts are resolved quickly, but some are not. Even in extreme cases, though, there is life after identity loss and consumers are usually able to straighten out their finances. Prevent ID theft from happening in the first place, but know that you can clean it up if the worst happens anyway.

CHAPTER

5

Win the New Mortgage Game

Just two or three years ago, it would have taken a whole book to explain the variety of choices in the mortgage market. There were 40-year, 30-year, 20-, 15-, and 10-year fixed-rate loans. There were adjustable-rate mortgages (ARMs) and adjustable-/fixed-rate hybrid mortgages—with every conceivable rate scheme and schedule. There were no-down-payment loans, and negative-amortization, interest-only, subprime option mortgages for people who couldn't afford any other loans. And there were no-documentation mortgages for people who didn't have any qualifying paperwork; in the business they were called "liar loans." It was a crazy time, and there was an abundance of money out there for every kind of mortgage you could imagine—and a few that you couldn't.

I think we all know how that turned out. When the housing bubble burst in 2006, it pulled many of those loans down with it, and led to a massive meltdown in the mortgage markets. By 2007, the subprime mortgage market had collapsed, with more than 25 lenders declaring bankruptcy, announcing big losses, or trying to put themselves up for sale. People who had taken out many of the newer adjustable-rate mortgages saw their monthly minimum payments rise to the point where they could no longer keep up with their loans—in many cases monthly payments doubled, or worse. In other cases, whole neighborhoods were wrecked by foreclosures and home prices that were falling faster than you can say "refinance." Even folks with good credit scores and solid jobs couldn't refinance into better and cheaper loans, because the outstanding balances on their mortgages were bigger than the new, lower values of their homes.

Mortgage money dried up, from the top and the bottom. The big buyers of mortgages, such as Fannie Mae and Freddie Mac, ran out of cash to buy new loans, as too many of the ones they already owned stopped earning them money. At the same time, consumers stopped wanting or qualifying for new loans. By the first quarter of 2009, a record 12 percent of homeowners were badly behind on their mortgage payments or in foreclosure.

The federal government stepped in with a host of plans to shore up both ends of the market. Trillions of dollars have flowed to the banks and the Wall Street buyers of mortgage-backed securities. New provisions allow homeowners to refinance or modify their mortgages, even if their loans are underwater (worth more than their homes) or in financial trouble.

And now, mortgages are coming back, but they look different. In fact, they look a lot like mortgages did in 1975 or 1980. All of those questionable and troubling interest-only, no-down-payment, option mortgages? Swept away. Some burdened homeowners still have them, but you couldn't get a new one, even if you wanted to. (You wouldn't.) Your choices today, if you go into a bank looking for a new loan, are basically for a fixed-rate loan or a conservative variable-rate loan. Keith Gumbinger of HSH Associates, a mortgage research firm, summed it up thus: "We have rebooted the entire mortgage lending system to what it would have been 20 years ago."

That means a return to mortgage basics. When you want to buy a home, the mortgage lender (typically a bank) will lend you the money to complete the purchase. You will own the home, but the lender will have a lien against it. The lender will own the loan. Typically, the lender will sell the loan to a secondary mortgage market player, like Fannie Mae or Freddie Mac. The new owner will package the mortgage, along with others, into mortgage-backed securities. They will pay a company—sometimes the same bank that made the loan in the first place—to service the loan by billing you monthly and collecting your payments. If you stay in your home long enough to pay off the mortgage, the lien will be dropped and you will own the home, free and clear.

This return to basics is not such a bad thing. As I write this, fixed rates on 30-year loans are hovering around 4.75 percent. That's very near their all-time low. There are far worse financial moves than getting a plain-vanilla 30-year fixed-rate mortgage for under 5 percent.

Whether you are in trouble with your existing mortgage or you just want to find the best new one, there are other strategies out there, too, for making the most of this new/old mortgage market. I'll review the best products out there now, as well as one more on the horizon. I'll teach you how to wring the most out of your home equity without putting your future at risk. In Chapter 10, I'll guide you through the mortgage modification and foreclosure options that can get you on solid ground. Here's what you need to know now to get, use, and pay off a mortgage.

Mortgage Troubles

If you're in trouble on your home loan, don't stop here. Go directly to Chapter 10, where I lay out, in detail, the various mortgage relief programs that have come out of the government in the past two years.

You can refinance your home, even if you've slipped underwater and your home is worth less than your current loan.

And you can modify your mortgage, if you need forbearance from the lender to stay in your house.

You have options, more than ever before. They are all there, in Chapter 10. Take heart.

How to Shop for a Mortgage

As soon as you know you're going to be in the market for a mortgage, get copies of your credit reports and your credit scores. Go back over Chapter 3, and do everything in your power to bolster your credit score—a solid score will save you big money!

Then read this entire chapter. It will give you guidance on what kind of mortgage is best for you. Once you've made that decision, get a few competitive offers. You can compare quotes from a local mortgage broker, a credit union or local bank, and a major national issuer as well as an online broker.

Use an online calculator to compare the offers you receive. There's no substitute for cold, hard numbers. A number of web sites offer great mortgage comparison tools, including amortization tables and calculators. If you're looking for a new loan, or trying to decide whether to refinance the one you've got, use these sites to see which option would actually save you the most money over the long term.

- HSH Associates, www.hsh.com/calc-amort.html
- Bankrate, www.bankrate.com
- Time Value Software, a long web address but worth it for a full-featured mortgage calculator that includes various types of mortgages, points, closing costs, and more: www.timevalue .com/calculators/mortgage-comparison-calculator.aspx

Here's a review of the different kinds of mortgages on the market now, and how to approach them.

The Safe Fixed-Rate Choice

Today, almost all mortgages being written are fixed-rate, fixed-term loans with very low rates. If you are looking for a new loan to buy a home, and have a good credit score and enough income to support your payments, or you have enough home equity to refinance, you should not have any trouble finding one of these loans. But even with these plain-vanilla loans there are trade-offs and decisions to be made.

Here are some of the items you should consider when shopping for a fixed-rate loan.

- **Rates versus points.** The lowest-cost loan isn't always the one with the lowest rate. It's the one that costs you the fewest dollars over your life with the loan. That means that it may be worth paying a point or two for a very low interest rate *if* you expect to keep the loan for a long time. Typically, you'll cut your interest rate by 0.25 percentage points for every 1 percent (one point) that you pay up front.
- **Length of the loan.** The longer the loan term, the smaller your monthly payments but the more you'll ultimately pay in interest. The shorter your loan, the lower the interest rate. For example, a 15-year loan will often be priced about 0.3 percentage points lower than a 30-year loan. Here's an example, for a $250,000 mortgage.

- A 30-year loan at 4.75 percent will require a monthly payment of $1,304. If you hold the loan for 30 years, you'll have paid $219,482 in interest over the life of the loan.
- A 15-year loan at 4.45 percent will require a monthly payment of $1,906. After 15 years you'll have paid off the loan, and $93,098 in interest.

Which one is better? That depends on you. In general, it is better to burn the mortgage early and free up your money for other expenses and investments. If you are nearing retirement, it makes sense to get the shorter loan. If you are just starting out and don't have a lot of disposable income, the longer loan might fit your family budget better.

- **Closing costs.** Some lenders will entice you with a low rate, but charge you so much on items like appraisal fees and photocopying costs that you'll end up paying more. See the accompanying box for more information about how to control your closing costs.
- **Affordability.** How much loan can you afford? The typical answer from bankers is this: Your housing expenses, including principal, interest, taxes, and insurance, should not be more than 30 percent of your pretax income. Your total monthly debt costs, including payments on the mortgage as well as car loans, student loans, and other installment loans, shouldn't be more than 40 percent of your monthly gross income.

Cut Closing Costs

Over-the-top closing costs can ruin even the best mortgage. Many lenders have a field day with the add-ons that come with a new loan. They pile on inflated and invented fees until you are paying thousands of dollars more than you thought, just for the privilege of borrowing money. On a smaller loan (less than $200,000), you can end up paying 3 percent of the total loan amount in closing costs.

The law requires lenders to give borrowers a good-faith estimate of what closing costs are expected to be with any loan application. But they aren't required to give you that until *after* you apply for the loan. Even then, their numbers can differ by hundreds or even thousands of dollars from the numbers they present to you at closing. You can fight that, and I'll tell you how in a minute.

(Continued)

The only real way to cut your closing costs is to break them down by line item and attack each individually. As you'll soon see, you can break out some items, such as appraisals, and comparison shop for them with different providers. You can negotiate the cost of others directly with your lender. If you get all the way to closing and then find new costs have popped up, don't be afraid to challenge them—even after you close. I have friends who received closing cost refunds simply because they took the time to send a letter of complaint to their mortgage company after their loan had closed.

One new Web-based company, Closing.com (www.closing.com) offers comparison shopping for the various services, such as appraisals and title insurance, that are included in closing costs. Here are some others, and ways to cut their costs:

- **Points.** It's often up to you to decide whether you'd rather pay more points for a lower rate.
- **Underwriting fees.** Yes, it's sad but true that lenders who are already earning interest and charging points also often charge fees for evaluating your mortgage application. Try to negotiate this fee away.
- **Administrative and document prep fees.** I call these the egregious fees. Try to negotiate them out of the deal. Why should you pay the cost of photocopying on top of all the other money you're paying the lender?
- **Wiring (or funding) fee.** Yes, this covers the actual cost of wiring the loan money to the closing attorney. Try to fight it.
- **Credit report fee.** Lenders will pull your credit reports and scores before deciding whether you are mortgageworthy, but they'll also often charge you a markup on what it actually costs them to get the reports.
- **Escrow (and nonescrow) fees.** Lenders usually collect your property taxes and homeowners' insurance payments as part of your monthly mortgage payment, and then forward them. But they may pay a third-party company to monitor that this account is being handled right. You can't win: If you say you want to pay your own taxes and insurance and carve them out of the monthly mortgage bill, they may raise your rate for that.
- **Appraisal fee.** You don't have to agree to the appraiser the lender wants. Ask if you can shop around.
- **Survey fee.** Lenders hire a third-party company to survey the property. Don't pay a markup on this; ask to see the receipt. If you're buying a condo, don't pay a survey fee.

- **Flood certification.** This is another outside service, and another one you shouldn't have to pay for if you're buying a condo.
- **Settlement or closing fee.** You will have to pay an attorney to handle the closing. Even if the seller provides the lawyer, you'll have to pay the bill, so it's good to find your own lawyer to handle the closing.
- **Title search.** You'll have to pay someone to go to the courthouse and look up the property.
- **Title insurance.** And then you'll have to buy title insurance anyway. You should definitely comparison shop this item. And, if you are refinancing or buying a home that has been in the seller's hands for less than 10 years, you may be able to get the current title insurance policy reissued at a rate far cheaper than a new policy.
- **Government fees.** You'll also have to pay county recording and tax fees in most places; it varies by jurisdiction, but isn't negotiable.

Adjustable-Rate Loans

There are dozens of varieties of adjustable-rate mortgage (ARM) loans, but right now, hardly anyone is applying for them.

The philosophy behind the ARM is this: If borrowers share the risk of rising interest rates with lenders, lenders can afford to lower the initial rates that borrowers pay. So, a typical spread between a 30-year fixed-rate loan and a 5/1 ARM (the rate is set for five years and then adjusts annually) is between 0.5 percentage point and 1 percentage point. Right now, as I'm writing this, the rates on 5/1 ARMs are 0.45 percentage points lower than the fixed-rate loans. The monthly payments on a $250,000 5/1 ARM would be $1,237; you would save $67 a month with the ARM—for the first five years. After that, there's no telling where rates would be and where your payment would go.

Traditionally, experts have told borrowers that ARMs make sense in an environment where home prices are rising, interest rates are high, the spreads between ARMs and fixed-rate mortgages are wide, and the borrower expects to move before the ARM starts to fluctuate.

This is not that environment! In fact, now is the opposite environment. I do not think ARMs are a good idea for any borrowers right now. With rates near their lows, ARMs are more likely to go up than down. People looking to move in five years may not even be able to sell their home then, and if they do, they may not get any more for it than it is worth today.

That being said, situations may change in the future. Many experts believe that once the economy starts to pick up, interest rates will rise swiftly. ARMs may start to make sense again. If you are considering taking out an adjustable-rate mortgage, here's what to consider.

- **Rate.** Make sure the spread between the ARM rate and the fixed rate is big enough to justify the extra risk.
- **Caps.** Most issuers offer two built-in caps to protect you from enormous increases in your payments. The *periodic rate cap* limits how much your payment can rise in any one adjustment. The *lifetime cap* limits the total increase in interest rates that you can face.
- **Amortization.** Some ARMs are not calculated to pay off over time; instead, they will leave you at the end of the mortgage with a balloon payment due. For example, the payments may be amortized over 30 years, but the loan is due in 10. That's dangerous. You have no idea what the mortgage market will be like then, when you'll have to replace your loan.
- **The payment.** Some ARMs also will cap your monthly payment, and defer increasing it over a preset level, even if interest rates go up. That's dangerous, too. You could end up never repaying your mortgage under those terms.
- **The index.** Different ARMs are linked to different interest rate indexes. They used to be linked to rates on Treasury bills and one-year Treasuries, but they are increasingly linked to the London Interbank Offered Rate (LIBOR). That is a very volatile index, and could cause the rate on your loan to jump around a bit.
- **The rules governing when the rate is reset.** Typically this happens once a year, but it can happen more often.
- **The period before rates are reset.** Some ARMs offer as long as 10 years before the rate resets. Five years is more typical; some require adjustments annually.

The ArcLoan—One Variable-Rate Loan That I Like

It may seem strange, after that last section, to admit that I have a variable-rate mortgage for my own house. But here's why: I have a variable-rate mortgage that can only go down, not up. It's called an ArcLoan, or automatic rate cut mortgage. I got my mortgage in February 2001 and the rate has fallen seven times since then.

Here's the concept behind it: Most mortgage lenders don't really want to lose customers when rates fall. By getting pre-agreement from the lenders to limit and then cover refinancing closing costs, ArcLoan customers are able to refinance whenever rates drop. The bankers win, because they keep their customers. The customers win, because they can take advantage of lower and lower rates without worrying about rate hikes, and without having to shop for new lenders every time rates fall.

The brains behind the ArcLoan are Keith Kelly and his brother Joe. They are about to come out with a new and improved version as well. Keith is developing what he calls the Harmony Loan. It will work like the ArcLoan, except that interest rate declines won't involve any actual behind-the-scenes refinances, as the ArcLoan does. It will instead give you, the borrower, the option of when to modify your mortgage whenever rates have dropped by at least a quarter of a percentage point from where they stood. It will cost less over time, because it won't involve the closing costs that regular ArcLoan refinancings incur. Keith is waiting for final government approval, but that may have come through by the time you read this book.

Should you go for an ArcLoan or Harmony Loan? Maybe and maybe not. It depends on what the rate environment is like when you are mortgage shopping, and on what kind of rates you can get on the Kelly brothers' products. But it's certainly worth a call for a quote. Here's how to find out about them.

- The ArcLoan
  www.arcloan.com
  (800) 272-5626
- The Harmony Loan
  www.mortgageharmony.com
  (800) 999-3764

Should You Refinance?

With mortgage rates near their historic lows, it is tempting to want to refinance your mortgage. You may be able to lock in a lower rate, or lower payments. Or refinance a long loan into a short loan, and kill your mortgage debt early. You may even be able to take money out of your home and pay off other high-interest-rate debts (though that is neither as easy nor as risk-free as it once was, given the sharp drop in home values).

You may be a good candidate for a refi loan if:

- You have a good credit score.
- You have a secure income and can afford the payments.
- You have equity in your home; that is, it is worth more than you owe on it.
- You still have many years to pay on your loan.
- Your loan is now at an above-market interest rate.

Of course, even if you don't fit those criteria, you might still want to refinance, and new government rules may allow you to (I'll get to them in a minute). But for now, traditional refinancers should consider this.

Sometimes a refinance can be a bad move. Say, for example, that you owe only 10 more years on a 6 percent loan. You could refinance for 30 years at 4 percent, but then you'd have to pay for 20 additional years—the refi would end up costing you a lot in interest, not to mention closing costs.

The rule of thumb used to be that it was worth refinancing only if you could cut your interest rate by two percentage points, but that no longer is valid. Now, some people find it worthwhile to refinance for only 0.5 percentage points.

There's no shortcut to answering this question; you have to do the math. Get some solid refinancing quotes, including closing costs, and ask yourself these questions:

- How will it affect my monthly payment?
- How will it affect my total payments over time?
- How will a new mortgage fit with my other financial goals? (For example, if a refinance would get your mortgage paid off before your kids go to college, that's a good thing. If it would spread your payments well into retirement, that might be a reason not to refinance.)
- What is the break-even point? (That is the year when you actually begin to save money by refinancing. Typically, the

addition of closing costs means that you actually spend money to refinance for the first few years. The bigger the rate differential between the new loan and the old loan, the quicker you'll break even.)

If your break-even point is much closer than the end of the time you expect to be in the house paying off the loan, then the refi is probably a good idea. One web site you should check to get a good deal on a refi is www.youcanrefi.com, or call them at 888-777-9682.

There are some excellent refinancing break-even calculators online. Here are a few of my favorites:

- **Financial Calculators:** www.dinkytown.net/java/Mortgage Refinance.html#calc
- **Bankrate:** www.bankrate.com/calculators/mortgages/refinance-calculator.aspx
- **HSH Associates Financial Publishers:** www.hsh.com/usnrcalc .html

Home Equity Lines

You can, of course, still get cash out of your home if you have equity in it, by getting a home equity line of credit (HELOC). These loans are still broadly available and heavily marketed; banks continue to make money on them. A HELOC is a revolving line of credit. You can draw whatever money you need from it. As long as you make a minimum monthly payment, usually the amount of interest that accrued in the previous month, you can pay back as much or as little as you want every month. You can run a balance.

A decent HELOC is a thing of beauty. It provides immediate emergency money if you need it. It's a low-interest (and often, fully tax-deductible) loan you can make to yourself. You can use it to repay high-interest debt, or as a low-cost substitute for expensive car, installment, or education loans. In the following chapter, you'll even learn of a great technique for using your HELOC to pay off your mortgage quickly and cheaply.

Of course, a HELOC is secured *by your house.* So, you don't want to borrow money via a HELOC if you are unsure about your ability to pay it back. And these lines all have variable rates, so a home equity debt that looks manageable at 5 percent can become unmanageable at 10 or 11 percent. You have to be careful not to borrow more than you can comfortably pay back.

But it's good to have a HELOC at your disposal. To line up a good one, shop at the same places where you would mortgage hunt: an online bank, your credit union, and your bank.

Look at these aspects of the line of credit before deciding which one to take:

- **The margin.** HELOCs typically are priced by adding a markup to the prime rate. The lower the markup (called the margin), the cheaper the loan over the long term. This is the single most important factor in the price of your loan. In some cases lenders will actually charge only the prime rate itself or even a quarter or a half point *below* prime.
- **The total amount of the line.** How much can you borrow? Not every lender will offer the same amount.
- **Closing costs.** These can be similar to the closing costs for a first mortgage, though many lenders will absorb more of the closing costs so the final expenses to the borrower won't seem so high. Many banks and credit unions are giving HELOCs away at no cost or a very low cost structure. Compare costs carefully.
- **The introductory rate and period.** If you need to borrow big right away, say to pay for a home renovation, you may benefit from a HELOC that has a very advantageous introductory rate. But typically, this is not a good reason to choose one loan over another. HELOCs are meant to last a long time—10 years or more—so a rate that lasts for only a few months, or even a year, doesn't mean much.
- **Minimum draws and balances.** Does the HELOC require that you use it? Keep a certain balance due? That's not good. You want to be able to use it as you need to, not borrow money you don't need to borrow just to keep the bank happy.
- **Draw rules.** How do you get money out of your HELOC? Can you transfer it directly to your checking account? Write checks on it? Is there a minimum amount you can borrow at a time? The more flexibility you have, the better.
- **Fees.** A minority of HELOCs tack on annual fees or cancellation fees: No and no. You're already paying closing costs and interest that should provide enough income for the lender.

You may have to pay a slightly higher interest rate, say 0.25 percentage points, to get a HELOC that doesn't include a cancellation fee.

Keep Your HELOC

Some lenders are tightening up their home equity lines of credit, even for borrowers in good standing. If you have a HELOC you're not using, use it, at least a little bit, to keep it active. If you don't have a HELOC and are afraid your job or credit situation might change for the worse, apply and secure the HELOC before you change jobs or do anything else that might hurt your credit score. Don't apply for any other credit, such as a new credit card, and don't miss any payments while you are in the process of applying for a HELOC. HELOC terms generally run 5, 10, 20, or 30 years with an interest-only payment and draw period of 5, 10, or 20 years. Now they commonly are written so that they last only 10 years, and then can be renewed by mutual agreement between the borrower and the lender. Others last for 15 years. If your HELOC is approaching the nine-year mark, you can start looking around for a new HELOC to replace it, just so you'll be armed with solid information about what's available before you have to renegotiate your existing line of credit with your bank.

Reverse Mortgages

You can also tap the equity in your home with a reverse mortgage, particularly if you are retired, own your home free and clear, and are at least 62 years old.

A reverse mortgage truly does work backwards: When you take out a reverse mortgage, you get a lump sum of cash, and you never have to make payments. However, as long as you live in and own the house, interest accrues. When the house is sold, the reverse mortgage must be paid off before any equity remaining goes to you (or your heirs).

Typically, older retirees who want to stay in their home, but need cash for home maintenance or personal care, choose to take reverse mortgages. If you do it when you are too young, you can run out of borrowing power before you run out of your need for money.

With a reverse mortgage, you can either get a lump sum of cash, or a line of credit, or a regular monthly payment called an annuity payment.

Some states even offer public reverse mortgages to elderly folks who want to tap their home equity to pay for their own long-term care. Some insurance companies have also paired reverse mortgages with annuities: You take out a reverse mortgage and turn the money you get over to an insurance company, which annuitizes it for you, insuring that it will last a lifetime. If you're interested in a deal like that, make very certain that all of the various fees built into that arrangement don't make it too costly to be worthwhile. And make sure that the monthly annuity payments you'd receive would fulfill your needs, because you'd be giving up the flexibility of withdrawing a larger sum in case of an emergency.

Reverse mortgages used to be so expensive as to be prohibitive. In some instances, they required homeowners to promise away large portions of their home's value to the lender. Fees for reverse mortgages typically topped $15,000, regardless of how small the loan was or how high the interest rate was. They have improved over the years, though it is still important that you comparison shop for a low-cost loan.

There are three very good sources of information on reverse mortgages. Check them all out thoroughly before you sign up for one.

1. **AARP.** The nation's foremost authority on reverse mortgages, Ken Scholen, created a special Reverse Mortgage Education Project for the AARP. It includes information about the latest wrinkles in reverse mortgage products, as well as a calculator that can give you an idea of how much money you can get from a reverse mortgage (www.aarp.org/money/personal/reverse_mortgages/).
2. **National Center for Home Equity Conversion.** Before he went to the AARP, Ken started this nonprofit to be an educational resource for all reverse mortgage customers. It's no longer kept up to date, but has lots of good information about how the reverse mortgage industry started and the regulations affecting the industry (www.reverse.org).
3. **National Reverse Mortgage Lenders Association.** Yes, it's the story told from the industry perspective, so consider the source. But this site also offers an excellent calculator and very solid information about how reverse mortgages work (www.reversemortgage.org).

Shared Equity Arrangements

There's one previously discredited home financing option that has come back to the market recently. Called shared equity arrangements, these deals occur when a homeowner receives a sum of money in return for a promise to repay that money, as well as a percentage of a home's appreciation between the time the homeowner takes the money and the time he or she eventually sells the house. Shared equity arrangements got a bad reputation when they were used, more than a decade ago, in the reverse mortgage market. Lenders often exacted a too-high share of a home's value in return for those reverse loans, and some elderly borrowers were ripped off.

But now, shared equity arrangements are back on the market and aimed at borrowers of every age. They have lower costs and more regulations than they used to.

These arrangements can be helpful to people who want to stay in their homes, need cash, and are more comfortable giving away part of their home appreciation than they are signing on to a traditional reverse mortgage. After all, if their home declines in value before they sell it, they may come away with more cash than they otherwise would have. (At least one of the companies in this space, Rex & Co., agrees to share in home depreciation as well as appreciation.)

But caution is in order. These arrangements may come laden with fees. With the cost of homes down all around the country, you may be signing away *a lot* of appreciation.

These three companies are currently offering shared equity (or shared appreciation) agreements.

1. **Rex & Company:** www.rexagreement.com
2. **Equity Key:** www.equitykey.com
3. **Grander Financial:** www.granderfinancial.com

Paying Off Your Mortgage Early

Even having a good mortgage—like a 30-year, low-interest, fixed-rate loan—is not as good as being mortgage free. People who pay off their loans early save thousands of dollars—sometimes hundreds of thousands of dollars—over the lives of their loans. They have more money in their pockets for their kids' college, for travel, for retirement, or for just about anything else.

If you want to pay off your mortgage early, first think about whether you would be a good candidate for that. Here are some questions to ask yourself before sending extra cash to your mortgage lender.

- Is this the best use of my extra cash?
- Do I have an emergency fund?
- Am I making regular contributions to my 401(k) plan and individual retirement account?
- Have I paid off other debt that carries a higher interest rate than my mortgage?
- If I am near retirement, will I still be left with enough cash if I pay off my loan?

If you answer yes to all of those questions, you are a good candidate for an aggressive mortgage-paydown program.

Make sure that your mortgage does not carry a prepayment penalty. Most don't. Then develop your own plan for how to best make extra payments regularly to your lender. Do not pay some company to manage your prepayment plan for you: A few years ago some firms (scam artists, really) made big bucks instituting bimonthly payment plans for homeowners. They made it sound like the bimonthly system was so complex you couldn't possibly do it yourself.

Of course you can. Here are three ways you can burn your mortgage early simply by sending extra cash to your lender.

1. **Bigger payments.** You can pay off your mortgage early simply by sending extra money to your mortgage company every month. Come up with a set amount and stick with it. You can go to an excellent mortgage payment calculator at Bankrate (www.bankrate.com) and see how this would work. Say, for example, you had a new $250,000, 30-year, 5 percent fixed-rate mortgage. Your monthly payment would be $1,342. If you sent in an additional $1,000 with every monthly payment, you'd pay off your loan in 12 years and save $151,733 in total interest payments.
2. **Windfall payments.** What if you can't afford to pay an extra $1,000 a month toward your mortgage, but you get a one-time $5,000 holiday bonus at work? Put that one payment toward

your mortgage just once, during the first year you hold the loan, and you'll ultimately pay it off 15 months early and save $16,000 in interest.

3. **Bimonthly payments.** Many people recommend this strategy for paying off your mortgage early: Split your monthly mortgage payment in two, and pay half of it every two weeks, for 26 payments during the year. Of course, that means you are making an extra month's payment every year, but it may not feel so burdensome.

Here are the financial consequences of that. If you take that same $1,342 monthly mortgage, split it in two, and pay $671 every two weeks, you'll pay off your loan in just over 25 years. You'll save $43,397 in interest over the life of the loan.

Sounds good, right? In the next chapter I explain an innovative new way in which you can use your home equity line to burn your mortgage even faster and easier. Read on.

CHAPTER

6

Mortgage Free in Five to Seven Years

Pssst—this whole chapter is a big secret, but it's one you are going to be very happy I am sharing with you. It's a secret that will more than pay for this book; you could use my secret to become *completely debt free* in less than a decade.

I'm talking about a new way to manage your mortgage, and your monthly cash flow, so that you—and not some banker—get to squeeze the most use out of every dollar that comes in and every dollar that goes out. Used correctly, this strategy will enable you to pay off your mortgage in as many years as some people take to pay off their cars.

The strategy is called equity acceleration, or mortgage acceleration. It's not such a big secret in Australia and the United Kingdom, where as many as one in four homeowners are accelerating their mortgages.

It's legal. It's not a scam. It's entirely aboveboard. Anyone with a decent credit score and good bill-management skills can accelerate the end of their mortgage and other debts by using the system I am going to lay out here.

Here is a basic outline of how it works:

- You finance a new home or refinance an existing one by obtaining a home equity line of credit (HELOC) requiring an interest-only monthly payment for at least 10 years.

- You use the HELOC to pay off your existing mortgage (if you have one). The HELOC replaces a new or existing conventional mortgage.
- You send your whole paycheck into the HELOC every time you are paid. This covers your monthly minimum payment, and then some. The HELOC becomes the new depository for your income.
- You pay your bills out of the HELOC, as close to the due date as possible. That maximizes the amount of time your money sits in the HELOC, cutting your interest.
- Any extra money you have left in the HELOC account after you pay your bills and make the minimum interest payment on the HELOC goes toward further accelerating your debt reduction every month.

Why It Works

The key to grasping the power of equity acceleration to eradicate your debt so quickly is understanding how interest is calculated in a traditional mortgage and in a HELOC. As you learned in the preceding chapter, a HELOC is a revolving loan. That gives you the flexibility to make interest-only minimum monthly payments every month, or to make larger payments if you want to.

In a traditional fixed-rate mortgage, the monthly principal and interest payment is predetermined and calculated according to a conventional amortization schedule, and the principal is assessed every month on an ascending schedule. With an average-sized 30-year conventional mortgage, it could take almost 19 years before more principal than interest is coming out of each monthly payment. You can, of course, pay the mortgage off early and reduce overall interest costs, but it isn't until you've completely paid off the loan that you realize the savings. There isn't an immediate benefit to you on a monthly basis; you are still obligated to make the original monthly payment, and all of the principal payments are locked away in your mortgage holder's treasure chest. And of course, they don't give you a key to their treasure chest.

A portion of your monthly payment is applied toward the outstanding balance of your loan and facilitates the payback of the debt. The remaining portion of your payment pays the interest you agreed to when you borrowed the money.

In a HELOC, interest is recalculated every month on the basis of the average daily balance of the principal owed. The more money you run through your line of credit (even if the deposits do not stay there long), the more you are driving down the principal and setting the stage for those interest costs to be calculated on a lower average daily balance. As the monthly interest is pushed down, more and more of your cash goes toward paying off the principal owed, and *that* results in lower and lower interest charges every month. That gets compounding working for you, instead of against you.

It's true that interest rates on HELOCs are variable, which means that this strategy operates in an open-ended, variable environment. That may sound scary, but in fact, the accelerator system is so powerful it even trumps rate increases. Bill Westrom, my guru on this strategy, helps consumers to accelerate the payoff of their mortgages through his company Truth in Equity (www.truthin equity.com). And he has found that even if interest rates on HELOCs rise to frightening, double-digit levels, the equity acceleration strategy creates a smaller bottom line and a faster debt payoff.

Here are a couple of case studies from his customer files that demonstrate how the equity accelerator can work.

Mark and Susan

Mark and Susan owned a home in Indiana. They had 12 years left on a 15-year mortgage with a fixed interest rate pegged at 5.25 percent. Their original mortgage was $225,000. After three years of making payments, they still owed $192,934 or 86 percent of the original loan amount. Their take-home monthly income was about $7,500 and their monthly expenses came in at $5,250, including their $1,809 mortgage payment. (See Figure 6.1.)

The couple was a good candidate for an equity accelerator because they had a substantial positive cash flow. They also had equity in their home, good credit scores, and, more important, a willingness to take an active role in managing and controlling their financial future.

The couple replaced their conventional mortgage with a new HELOC.

As the principal on the HELOC began to drop, their interest costs also have gone down and their monthly cash flow has improved. Every month, more of their extra cash flow goes to paying down the loan.

Original Loan Amount: $225,000						
Remaining Term: 12 years						

Current Economic Structure

Mortgages	Balance	Payment	Interest Rate	Expenses		
1st Mortgage	$192,934.45	$1,808.72	5.25%	Monthly Living Expenses	$3,191.00	
2nd Mortgage	$0.00	$0.00	0.00%	Total Monthly Expenses	$5,249.72	
Monthly Tax & Ins		$250.00				
Totals	$192,934.45	$2,058.72		Income		
				Deposited Net Income	$7,500.00	
				Investment Income	$0.00	
No vehicle or credit card				Other Income	$0.00	
debt to report				Totals	$7,500.00	

Conventional 15-Year Amortization					
Currently in Year 3					
End of Year	Loan Balance	Payment	Accumulated Interest	Accumulated Principal	Liquid Funds
Opening Balance	$225,000.00	$1,808.72	$ 0.00	$ 0.00	$0.00
1	$214,866.26	$1,808.72	$ 11,570.96	$ 10,133.74	$0.00
2	$204,187.52	$1,808.72	$ 22,596.92	$ 20,812.48	$0.00
3	$192,934.45	$1,808.72	$ 33,048.54	$ 32,065.55	$0.00
4	$181,076.17	$1,808.72	$ 42,894.96	$ 43,923.83	$0.00
5	$168,580.13	$1,808.72	$ 52,103.62	$ 56,419.87	$0.00
6	$155,412.02	$1,808.72	$ 60,640.21	$ 69,587.98	$0.00
7	$141,535.72	$1,808.72	$ 68,468.60	$ 83,464.28	$0.00
8	$126,913.11	$1,808.72	$ 75,550.70	$ 98,086.89	$0.00
9	$111,504.08	$1,808.72	$ 81,846.37	$113,495.92	$0.00
10	$ 95,266.32	$1,808.72	$ 87,313.31	$129,733.68	$0.00
11	$ 78,155.27	$1,808.72	$ 91,906.95	$146,844.73	$0.00
12	$ 60,123.94	$1,808.72	$ 95,580.32	$164,876.06	$0.00
13	$ 41,122.86	$1,808.72	$ 98,283.94	$183,877.14	$0.00
14	$ 21,099.87	$1,808.72	$ 99,965.65	$203,900.13	$0.00
15	$ 0.00	$ 0.00	$100,570.47	$225,000.00	$0.00

Figure 6.1   Mark and Susan's Conventional 15-Year Mortgage and Year-to-Year Amortization Results

Now, instead of looking at 12 years, the couple is on track to be mortgage free in 4 years and 10 months and save over $45,000 in interest costs. (See Figure 6.2.)

You can see exactly how that will work by comparing the amortization tables in Figures 6.1 and Figure 6.2. Figure 6.1 shows how Mark and Susan would have paid off their 15-year loan. Figure 6.2 shows how they are blowing through their debt in under five years instead.

Megan and Jared

Here's another quite different example of how the system can work for a Manhattan couple who don't have the extra cash flow that Mark and Susan enjoy.

Megan, at 35, earns a salary of $75,000 as an editor at a New York publishing house, and her husband earns $90,000 as an art director.

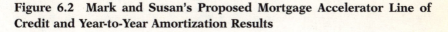

Current Economic Structure						
Mortgages	**Balance**	**Payment**		**Expenses**		
1st Mortgage	$192,934.45	$1,808.72		Monthly Living Expenses		$3,191.00
2nd Mortgage	$0.00	$0.00		Total Monthly Expenses		$5,249.72
Monthly Tax & Ins		$250.00				
Totals	$192,934.45	$2,058.72		**Income**		
				Deposited Net Income		$7,500.00
No vehicle or credit card debt to report				Investment Income		$0.00
				Other Income		$0.00
				Totals		$7,500.00

Proposed Mortgage Accelerator Line of Credit

Proposed Loan Amount	$221,250.00			
Proposed Interest Rate	4.00%			
		New Line of Credit		
		Line Amount	$221,250.00	
		Consolidation Balance	$192,934.45	
Debt Restructure		**Reallocation**		
1st Mortgage	$192,934.45	Liquid Assets	$0.00	
2nd Mortgage	$0.00			
Credit Card Debt	$0.00			**1st Month**
Installment Debt	$0.00	**1st Month Balance**	$192,934.45	**Payment Savings**
Total	$192,934.45	**1st Month Payment**	$643.11	
				$1,415.61

Mortgage Accelerator Amortization						
Projected Payoff: 4 years, 8 months						
End of Year	Loan Balance	Payment	Accumulated Interest	Accum. Payment Savings vs. 15-yr Mtg. (PITI)	Available Liquid Funds	
Opening Balance	$192,934.45	$643.11	$ 643.11	$ 1,415.61	$ 28,315.55	
1	$155,273.13	$582.27	$ 7,320.40	$ 17,384.24	$ 65,976.87	
2	$113,408.01	$519.79	$13,950.79	$ 35,458.49	$107,205.70	
3	$ 70,268.86	$380.62	$19,072.99	$ 55,040.93	$150,981.14	
4	$ 25,246.68	$157.79	$22,063.10	$ 76,755.46	$196,003.32	
5	$ 0.00	$ 0.00	$22,459.62	$101,063.58	$221,250.00	
6						
7						
8						
9						
10						
11						
12						
13						
14						
15						

Figure 6.2 Mark and Susan's Proposed Mortgage Accelerator Line of Credit and Year-to-Year Amortization Results

The balance of Megan's inheritance—$50,000—is in a mutual fund that has been returning an average of 8 percent a year.

Megan and Jared bought a co-op in the upper west corner of Manhattan five years ago in Hudson Heights, where real estate prices aren't nearly as high as further downtown. They put $75,000 down on a co-op costing $475,000.

They have 25 years left on their mortgage, which has a fixed interest rate of 6.25 percent. Their combined take-home pay is $9,000 a month. Their monthly mortgage payment is $2,463. When you add in their commuting and parking costs and other expenses, there isn't much money left at the end of the month.

| Original Loan Amount: $400,000 |
| Remaining Term: 25 years |

| Current Economic Structure |

Mortgages	Balance	Payment	Interest Rate	Expenses	
1st Mortgage	$373,348.97	$2,462.87	6.25%	Monthly Living Expenses	$3,575.00
2nd Mortgage	$0.00	$0.00	0.00%	Total Monthly Expenses	$6,637.87
Monthly Tax & Ins		$600.00			
Totals	$373,348.97	$3,062.87		Income	
				Deposited Net Income	$9,000.00
				Investment Income	$0.00
				Other Income	$0.00
No vehicle or credit card debt to report				Totals	$9,000.00

| | Conventional 30-Year Amortization | | | | |
| | Megan and Jared Currently in Year 5 | | | | |
End of Year	Loan Balance	Payment	Accumulated Interest	Accumulated Principal	Liquid Funds
Opening Balance	$400,000.00	$2,462.87	$ 0.00	$ 0.00	$0.00
1	$395,312.82	$2,462.87	$ 24,867.24	$ 4,687.18	$0.00
2	$390,324.15	$2,462.87	$ 49,433.00	$ 9,675.85	$0.00
3	$385,014.60	$2,462.87	$ 73,677.87	$ 14,985.40	$0.00
4	$379,363.52	$2,462.87	$ 97,581.23	$ 20,636.48	$0.00
5	$373,348.97	$2,462.87	$121,121.09	$ 26,651.03	$0.00
6	$366,947.54	$2,462.87	$144,274.09	$ 33,052.46	$0.00
7	$360,134.36	$2,462.87	$167,015.34	$ 39,865.64	$0.00
8	$352,882.95	$2,462.87	$189,318.36	$ 47,117.05	$0.00
9	$345,165.11	$2,462.87	$211,154.94	$ 54,834.89	$0.00
10	$336,950.85	$2,462.87	$232,495.11	$ 63,049.15	$0.00
11	$328,208.23	$2,462.87	$253,306.91	$ 71,791.77	$0.00
12	$318,903.27	$2,462.87	$273,556.38	$ 81,096.73	$0.00
13	$308,999.80	$2,462.87	$293,207.34	$ 91,000.20	$0.00
14	$298,459.32	$2,462.87	$312,221.28	$101,540.68	$0.00
15	$287,240.86	$2,462.87	$330,557.24	$112,759.14	$0.00
16	$275,300.80	$2,462.87	$348,171.61	$124,699.20	$0.00
17	$262,592.74	$2,462.87	$365,017.98	$137,407.26	$0.00
18	$249,067.27	$2,462.87	$381,046.94	$150,932.73	$0.00
19	$234,671.83	$2,462.87	$396,205.91	$165,328.17	$0.00
20	$219,350.43	$2,462.87	$410,438.95	$180,649.57	$0.00
21	$203,043.54	$2,462.87	$423,686.48	$196,956.46	$0.00
22	$185,687.76	$2,462.87	$435,885.13	$214,312.24	$0.00
23	$167,215.63	$2,462.87	$446,967.42	$232,784.37	$0.00
24	$147,555.33	$2,462.87	$456,861.55	$252,444.67	$0.00
25	$126,630.45	$2,462.87	$465,491.09	$273,369.55	$0.00
26	$104,359.64	$2,462.87	$472,774.71	$295,640.36	$0.00
27	$ 80,656.34	$2,462.87	$478,625.83	$319,343.66	$0.00
28	$ 55,428.39	$2,462.87	$482,952.31	$344,571.61	$0.00
29	$ 28,577.74	$2,462.87	$485,656.08	$371,422.26	$0.00
30	$ 0.00	$ 0.00	$486,632.77	$400,000.00	$0.00

Figure 6.3   Megan and Jared's Conventional 30-Year Mortgage and Year-to-Year Amortization Results

During the five years they've owned the apartment, Megan and Jared have sent their mortgage company over $147,000 in principal and interest payments; of that, $121,121 was interest and $26,651 was applied toward principal. They still owe over $373,348 or 93 percent of their original mortgage! If they continue on this path for the next seven years, after 12 years of payments they will still owe $318,903. (See Figure 6.3.) They would have absorbed an additional $152,000 in interest costs, and would still have 216 more payments before they would be mortgage free.

Current Economic Structure					
Mortgages	**Balance**	**Payment**		**Expenses**	
1st Mortgage	$373,348.97	$2,462.87		Monthly Living Expenses	$3,575.00
2nd Mortgage	$0.00	$0.00		Total Monthly Expenses	$6,637.87
Monthly Tax & Ins		$600.00			
Totals	$373,348.97	$3,062.87		**Income**	
				Deposited Net Income	$9,000.00
No vehicle or credit card debt to report				Investment Income	$0.00
				Other Income	$0.00
				Totals	$9,000.00

Proposed Mortgage Accelerator Line of Credit

Proposed Loan Amount	$450,000.00
Proposed Interest Rate	4.00%

New Line of Credit	
Line Amount	$450,000.00
Consolidation Balance	$373,348.97
Reallocation	$0.00
Liquid Assets	

Debt Restructure	
1st Mortgage	$373,348.97
2nd Mortgage	$0.00
Credit Card Debt	$0.00
Installment Debt	$0.00
Total	$373,348.97

		1st Month Payment Savings
1st Month Balance	$373,348.97	
1st Month Payment	$1,244.49	
		$1,818.38

Mortgage Accelerator Amortization Projected Payoff: 8 years, 6 months						
End of Year	Loan Balance	Payment	Accumulated Interest	Accum. Payment Savings vs. 30-yr Mtg. (PITI)	Available Liquid Funds
Opening Balance	$373,348.97	$1,244.49	$ 1,244.49	$ 1,818.38	$ 76,651.03
1	$334,500.96	$1,254.38	$ 14,882.34	$ 21,872.10	$115,499.04
2	$292,499.36	$1,340.62	$ 30,506.98	$ 43,001.90	$160,960.41
3	$250,800.66	$1,358.50	$ 45,988.16	$ 64,275.16	$199,199.34
4	$209,383.38	$1,308.65	$ 61,286.13	$ 85,731.63	$240,616.62
5	$167,425.51	$1,185.93	$ 75,553.89	$108,218.31	$282,574.49
6	$124,028.22	$ 981.89	$ 87,863.34	$132,663.30	$325,971.78
7	$ 78,172.40	$ 684.01	$ 97,160.95	$160,120.13	$371,827.60
8	$ 28,665.12	$ 274.71	$102,213.24	$191,822.28	$421,334.88
9	$ 0.00	$ 0.00	$102,836.90	$206,512.97	$450,000.00
10					
11					
12					
13					
14					
15					

Figure 6.4 Megan and Jared's Proposed Mortgage Accelerator Line of Credit and Year-to-Year Amortization Results

Megan and Jared have a couple of options if they are to take advantage of the equity accelerator concept.

If they simply refinance their current mortgage into an equity accelerator, and Megan keeps her $50,000 inheritance in a mutual fund, they could be debt free in eight and a half years. (See Figure 6.4.) This would save them over $262,675 in additional interest costs and their mortgage would be paid off. (In comparison, with their current mortgage, Megan and Jared would still owe $303,811 of the original balance and $183,836 in additional interest costs at that time.)

If Megan decides to close out her mutual fund and apply those funds toward an equity accelerator line of credit, Megan and Jared

Current Economic Structure						
Mortgages	**Balance**	**Payment**		**Expenses**		
1st Mortgage	$373,348.97	$2,462.87		Monthly Living Expenses	$3,575.00	
2nd Mortgage	$0.00	$0.00		Total Monthly Expenses	$6,637.87	
Monthly Tax & Insurance		$600.00				
Totals	$373,348.97	$3,062.87		**Income**		
				Deposited Net Income	$9,000.00	
No vehicle or credit card debt to report				Investment Income	$0.00	
				Other Income	$0.00	
				Totals	$9,000.00	

Proposed Mortgage Accelerator Line of Credit		
Proposed Loan Amount	$450,000.00	
Proposed Interest Rate	4.00%	

New Line of Credit	
Line Amount	$450,000.00
Consolidation Balance	$373,348.97

Debt Restructure		**Reallocation**	
1st Mortgage	$373,348.97	Mutual Fund	$50,000.00
2nd Mortgage	$0.00		
Credit Card Debt	$0.00		**1st Month Payment Savings**
Installment Debt	$0.00	**1st Month Balance** $323,348.97	
Total	$373,348.97	**1st Month Payment** $1,077.83	$1,985.04

Mortgage Accelerator Amortization with $50,000 Mutual Fund Contribution Projected Payoff: 6 years, 9 months					
End of Year	Loan Balance	Payment	Accumulated Interest	Accum. Payment Savings vs. 30-yr Mtg. (PITI)	Available Liquid Funds
Opening Balance	$323,348.97	$1,077.83	$ 1,077.83	$ 1,985.04	$126,651.03
1	$282,528.98	$1,059.48	$12,715.47	$ 24,038.97	$167,471.02
2	$237,868.42	$1,090.23	$25,625.65	$ 47,883.23	$215,342.09
3	$192,944.37	$1,045.12	$37,818.48	$ 72,444.84	$257,055.63
4	$147,498.72	$ 921.87	$49,014.69	$ 98,003.07	$302,501.28
5	$100,570.76	$ 712.38	$58,225.59	$125,546.61	$349,429.24
6	$ 51,083.34	$ 404.41	$64,340.98	$156,185.66	$398,916.66
7	$ 0.00	$ 0.00	$66,157.50	$191,123.58	$450,000.00
8					
9					
10					
11					
12					
13					
14					
15					

Figure 6.5   Megan and Jared's Proposed Mortgage Accelerator Line of Credit, $50,000 Mutual Fund Contribution, and Year-to-Year Amortization Results

would own their home outright in only six years, nine months, and would save an additional $36,679 in interest charges and be mortgage free. (See Figure 6.5.)

Got the concept? What the accelerator system does is funnel more of your money into debt reduction and set the stage for you to benefit from this immediately. By converting your lazy money— that's money sitting in accounts without connection to your home equity, such as a checking account—into money that works to pay off your mortgage, you reduce the amount you owe. That cuts your interest costs and hastens the day when your mortgage is but a distant memory.

It's Not for Everyone

The mortgage acceleration concept won't work for everyone. Like the other strategies in this book, it requires discipline. You have to be a smart cash-flow manager to make it work. You also have to have high enough credit scores to get a good HELOC, and confidence that your income stream will continue. Implementing this strategy will improve your cash flow from day one, but it may not be enough to mitigate the affects of a variable rate loan. This is why I recommend a thorough analysis of your personal finances by a qualified expert before blindly implementing this strategy.

If you decide to implement the equity accelerator concept with one of my recommended suppliers, you may be charged for the cost of the software, closing costs associated with the new loan, or a consultation fee. You won't be able to do this without any costs, but done right, the system will be profitable.

The risks of mortgage acceleration are these: If you fall back into conventional practice, relying on your checking account for deposits and bill paying, you defeat the purpose of the strategy and could extend the life of your debt instead of paying it off quickly. If you aren't disciplined about paying your bills on time out of your HELOC, you could end up with late fees. If you lose your job and the extra cash flow that makes the mortgage acceleration system work, that leaves you dependent on that open-ended variable-rate environment. If interest rates then rise, you could end up going backwards.

However, if there is a disruption in income, you can rely on the available equity in the HELOC to sustain your lifestyle until income is restored. In this scenario the acceleration process will be interrupted, but you won't find yourself in a stressful situation wondering how to make ends meet.

And yet, there are rewards even beyond the big one of doing away with your mortgage very quickly. You can run other debts through your HELOC as well. Do you have some expensive credit card debt sticking around? A costly car loan? You can use this acceleration strategy even if you don't have a conventional mortgage—if you simply have a lot of consumer debt or a big HELOC balance you'd like to burn through quickly. If you have a fixed-rate long-term mortgage with a very low interest rate and a big HELOC balance, you can leave the fixed-rate mortgage alone and simply use this technique to get the HELOC paid off before interest rates rise.

And, ready for this, once the HELOC is paid off you can utilize the equity in the HELOC to accelerate the pay off of your conventional mortgage. The HELOC is a very powerful tool once you know how to use it.

The biggest benefit of running your family finances through your HELOC is flexibility. It puts you in charge of your money, *not* some faceless mortgage banker. If money is a little tight one month, you don't have to worry about how the bills will get paid. Life will go on as usual. The principal balance on the HELOC won't be reduced as much as in the previous month, but the money will be there to cover your expenses. If you get a raise, you can put the extra money to work in your HELOC every paycheck. If you make extra payments on your traditional mortgage and then need the money back for an emergency, you're in trouble: Mortgage bankers don't give refunds. If you make extra payments to your HELOC and then have an emergency, you can simply write yourself a check to cover it, because it is a revolving line of credit. This is the beauty of this strategy; you maintain absolute freedom and authority over your finances.

This strategy can be especially useful at a time like this, because the alternatives for your extra cash don't look great. Today money market mutual funds and banks are paying less than 1 percent interest for your savings. It's hard to think of a place where you can earn more money on your cash than it can earn by working to pay off your mortgage early.

Do It Right

The concept behind mortgage acceleration is beautifully simple, but the execution can be complex. Here are some pointers for doing it right.

- **You have to get the right loan.** Until the recent credit crisis, there were a couple of special mortgage lenders in the United States who were specialists in the HELOC mortgage acceleration market. These special lenders offered long (20 years or more) draw and payoff periods and very facile checking and transfer privileges. Unfortunately, those accounts have dried up and are not widely available. Here's hoping that they come back. In the meantime, you have to find yourself a decent HELOC. You can go back to the previous chapter to see how to do that.

- **You have to set up easy transfers.** Because accelerator HELOCs don't exist right now, you have to do most of the transferring yourself. That means setting up a HELOC that links quickly with your checking account, so you can be moving money into your HELOC as soon as you get paid, and moving it back out only when you have to pay a bill. Often it is possible to set up your checking account at the same bank that gave you the HELOC. It helps to have a HELOC with broad check-writing privileges. That way you can pay your bills on time with a HELOC check and get a few more days of float in your loan account before the check clears.

- **You have to make sure that you're using the HELOC as the primary depository for your income.** Of course, if you continually draw too much money back out, you'll go backward instead of forward. The system works best when the monthly surplus (income less expenses) is continually applied toward the outstanding balance of the HELOC every month. That mitigates the interest cost and reduces the principal.

- **Can you do this for yourself?** Absolutely, if you're driven and disciplined. You must have a rudimentary understanding of current HELOCs so you can obtain the proper financing. You must also understand how to effectively deposit income and pay expenses if you want to get the most out of this program. I recommend that you hire an expert to make sure you have all of the right pieces and the moving parts in the proper sequence.

Suggested Companies

There are four companies listed here, and I think it's pretty obvious that I have my favorite. However, you should check in with all of them and see which one offers the best combination of service and cost to please you.

1. **Truth in Equity (www.truthinequity.com).** At Truth in Equity, Bill Westrom and his colleagues take a holistic approach in the analysis and evaluation of your family's financial situation and decide whether mortgage acceleration makes sense for you. If you go ahead with the program, his company will prepare spreadsheets and specific directions to help you accelerate your accelerator, so to speak. His firm acts as consultants. I like

that, because it provides you with a dedicated staff to protect you from making a poor financial decision, and they are there to help you achieve the projected payoff goal. Every month, Bill and his colleagues will monitor your activity and evaluate your performance. This monthly counseling session will help identify any weaknesses in your performance so you can make corrections and maintain the course to a debt-free life.

I do recommend this particular program, because I know Bill and have seen his spreadsheets. I like his hand-holding, consulting model. I know it works.

2. **The Money Merge Account (www.unitedfirstfinancial.com/moneymergepage.html).** United First Financial is a software company that sells equity accelerator software through agents and offers coaching to homeowners who want to use this debt-reduction system.

3. **No More Mortgage (www.nomoremortgage.com).** This firm also offers the mortgage acceleration alternative, and it sells other debt consolidation and elimination plans as well. It is a multilevel marketing company that basically sells the software you can use to design your own mortgage acceleration plan.

4. **Harj Gill's Speed Equity (www.speedequity.com).** Harj Gill, another player in this same market, got his start in Australia, where these products have a longer history. Learn more from his book, *Own Your Home Years Sooner* (American Mortgage Eliminators Publishing, 2003).

Broaden Your Scope

Once you've gotten the mortgage acceleration plan down, there is a lot you can do with it. As long as your line of credit is sufficiently large, you can consolidate all of your other debts into it, and get completely debt free faster than you thought possible. You can pay off your home in five to seven years, and then with this new heightened level of financial expertise you can use your HELOC to buy a second vacation or retirement home. (Don't look now, but real estate prices are pretty attractive.)

You can also self-finance your next car, self-finance your next tuition bill, or start that side business without having to fill out a million forms and beg some banker. You can be your own banker now. I *told* you it would be a good secret!

CHAPTER

7

Credit Cards: Just Because It's Called MasterCard Doesn't Mean It's the Boss of You

I probably get more calls, e-mails, and letters about credit cards than about any other issue. So many people are in over their heads with credit card balances that seem to grow with every statement. Consumers who think they are doing the right thing complain that they are getting tripped up by hidden fees, punitive rate hikes, "gotcha" billing practices, and other strategies that card issuers use to separate their customers from their cash.

The card companies have been running the table for a long time, and they've made a bundle by betting that consumers won't be able to find their way through the confusing terms they've built into their plastic. This is a big deal. In 2008, consumers paid $130 billion in interest and fees to credit card issuers, according to R. K. Hammer, an independent analyst who follows the industry. And he expects more fees in the future.

It would be nice for consumers to keep that money in their own pockets, and believe me, there are some great strategies for beating the card companies at their own game. You can play gotcha right back at them, if you've got the right information and the right attitude. That's what I'm here to tell you.

You can actually make money on your credit cards if you know how to find the best cards and how to use them, how to protect yourself from the industry's onerous fees and billing practices, and how to make the most out of the attractive bonuses and givebacks they offer. You need to know the best techniques for paying off credit card balances and grabbing the free money that issuers will sometimes leave on the table for you.

I'll lay all of that out in this chapter. But first—how did we get here? And where are we?

A Look at the Landscape

The credit card as we know it now is only 50 years old. In 1959, American Express introduced the first plastic card, and that same year, Bank of America allowed users of its card to revolve—or carry a balance—from one month to the next.

After that it was off to the races, and the growth in the use of credit cards has been nothing short of explosive. That was made easier with the role played since the mid-1960s by the massive payment-processing firms Visa and MasterCard, which create and run credit card programs. These two companies license their credit card plans to issuers, including banks and retailers, who brand them with their own names as well as the MasterCard or Visa logo. American Express and Discover are the third and fourth big credit card players; they brand and issue their own cards.

Today, there are roughly 1.5 billion credit cards in use in the United States; that's roughly eight cards for every adult in the country. Some 8 of every 10 U.S. households now have at least one credit card, and more than half—around 55 percent—regularly carry at least one credit card balance from one month into the next.

At first, consumers used credit cards for significant and irregular purchases like a refrigerator or a winter coat. But as technology advanced and credit card processing became easier and cheaper to do, the card issuers began encouraging consumers to use their plastic for everything from their 7-Eleven cup of coffee to their weekly groceries.

Flush on fee income and high interest payments, the issuers also began encouraging consumers to apply for and carry an expanding array of cards. In 2007, some 5.2 million card offers were mailed to consumers, according to tallying done by the Synovate Mail Monitor report. Issuers created hundreds of new cards with hundreds of new rewards programs designed to entice consumers into using their cards over and over and over.

Consumers complied in almost every way. They took on more and more cards, used them more and more widely, and slipped into revolving more and more of their balances. More than 23 billion credit card transactions were processed in the United States in 2007. Take a look at how credit card balances have grown in this country, according to data from the Federal Reserve Board of Governors and Credit.com:

- 1967: $1.4 billion
- 1977: $39 billion
- 1987: $169 billion
- 1997: $555 billion
- 2007: $972 billion

Yikes!

Then the credit crisis of 2008 hit. Rising unemployment met already-strapped consumers and they stopped paying their bills on time. By 2009, delinquencies (payments more than 60 days late) were at record high levels.

So the banks, already in trouble for making too many bad mortgage loans, started to rein in their credit card offers. Instead of the ever-expansive attitude they have had until now, they are making it harder for consumers to use their credit cards. They've cut their card solicitations and pulled back credit lines on existing cards, and they're getting tougher with their criteria of whom they will lend to at all. And sneaking more fees and higher rates into their bills.

At around the same time, the government stepped in. At the very end of 2008, the Federal Reserve Board—which regulates most credit card–issuing banks—set new rules designed to clamp down on some of these behaviors. Those rules don't go into effect until July 2010. Impatient with the pace of the Fed's rules, Congress passed its own Credit Cardholders' Bill of Rights Act of 2009. It doesn't become fully effective until the end of February 2010. Later in this chapter, I'll get into how all of these new rules and policies will affect the ways in which you use your cards.

This is where we are now: watching card companies get ever more aggressive until the new rules kick in. The current credit card landscape has become one big contradiction: There are too many cards, and too little credit. There is a wealth of great card offers, each with its own unique package of hidden fees and costs. Consumers owe too much but need to keep up with the new offers and continue using credit cards.

It's no wonder there's so much contradictory and confusing advice out there. Well, here's the straight story—the one central truth about credit cards that will lead you out of the confusion, away from the contradictions, and toward the best possible strategy for you:

> **There are two credit card worlds: one for people who carry balances and one for people who don't.**

Balance carriers have to approach credit cards one way, and balance payers have to approach them a whole other way.

It's not overstating the case to say that the balance payers are the winners of the credit card game. They get cash back on everything they buy, reap extra discounts from their issuers, load up on airline miles, and borrow money at zero percent interest every month of their lives. It says something that people in the credit card industry actually refer to these customers (privately, of course) as "deadbeats" or "freeloaders."

Anyone who carries a balance is actually subsidizing these so-called deadbeats. The revolvers (I'm not going to call them losers; maybe saps?) are the ones who are always getting caught by rising fees, rising rates, rising balances, and the stress of never being in the black.

Your goal, then, should be to become a credit card winner (a so-called deadbeat)—a person who never carries credit card debt unless it's at zero percent interest and you've planned it that way. Later in this chapter, I'll show you the best, quickest way to kill your credit card balances. But for now, here's how to get started in your new life as a credit card winner, even if you're still carrying a balance. Here's how to manage credit cards so that you are the master of them, and not vice versa.

Finding the Best Card(s) for You

Did you know that there are more than 1,250 unique credit cards out there? Even after cutting back on their solicitations, card issuers still are sending out roughly 100 million offers every single day. So there's got to be a good card out there for you, regardless of your situation. The trick is finding the right one—or ones. You can't always get everything you need out of one card, and the one that's been in your wallet for the past five years may not be the best one for right now. Here's how to find the right fit. (Note that I've included examples of some of the good deals that are out there right now. But because card offers change frequently, you should shop online to make sure you have the most current offers.)

Start Your Search

Use these web sites to begin hunting for the best cards that suit your situation. Each does an excellent job of surveying the credit card landscape and keeping up with the latest offers.

- www.creditcardperks.com
- www.credit.com
- www.indexcreditcards.com
- http://lowcards.com

- **If you usually carry balances.** Forget the fancy stuff; just hunt for the lowest-interest-rate, lowest-fee card you can find. The average interest rate for all cards now is just under 14 percent, according to IndexCreditCards (www.indexcreditcards.com), but there are some that are quite a bit lower. The Simmons First National Bank Visa Platinum Card (800-636-5151), for example, has a 7.25 percent fixed rate for cardholders with good credit scores. The Iberia Bank Gold Visa (800-980-2265) has an 8 percent fixed rate. If you're carrying a $5,000 balance on a card charging 18 percent interest, you'll save $42 every month by switching to an 8 percent card. You can boost those savings by getting a card that has a special zero percent one-year introductory rate, but only if it's permanent rate thereafter remains low.
- **If you don't usually carry balances but you have one now.** Look for one of the few zero percent balance transfer offers that are still out there. Move the balance to it, and set up your payments

so that you'll pay off the card before the zero percent ends. Beware of one pitfall: Most charge an up-front balance transfer fee of 3 percent of the balance. A few (such as the State Farm Good Neighbor Credit Card) eliminate that fee if you do the balance transfer quickly after getting the card. If you find yourself nearing the end of the zero balance period and still carrying this balance, look for another card to move the balance to.

- **If you always pay your balance off every month.** Good for you! You are free to make the most of all of the card rewards and freebies the industry has to throw at you. Later in this chapter, I'll tell you how to sort through all of the cash-back, free-mileage, gas-discount deals so that you can grab the maximum rewards from your cards. But for now, here's a strategy that will work for you: Don't worry about the interest rate. Look for cards that offer generous reward programs without charging any annual fees.

- **If you have problems on your credit report or a low credit score.** Can't get one of the good cards that are out there? Build your credit slowly with a secured credit card. To get a secured card, you have to deposit enough money with the card issuer to pay for your "credit." A deposit of $500, for example, will get you a secured credit limit of $500. As you use the card and make payments, the issuer will report your payment history to the credit bureaus. After a year of using a secured card, your credit report should be good enough to qualify you for a regular, unsecured credit card. There are, of course, pitfalls with these cards. If you are looking for a secured credit card, look for one that keeps fees in check. A $50 annual fee for the privilege of borrowing your own money may seem unreasonable, but it is pretty typical right now. And make sure that the issuer you deal with will report your payments to all three major credit bureaus.

How Many Cards Should You Have?

How many cards to have depends on you. If you really have no faith in your own ability to be disciplined about your spending and bill-paying habits, then keep it to one card, and use that card only for emergencies.

But work on your discipline! Cards can be very useful tools, and once you master them, you can have some fun with them, using different cards for different deals. One of my colleagues, Scott Bilker, who runs the DebtSmart web site (www.debtsmart.com), has made a career out of juggling the plastic. He and his wife have over 80 different credit cards! You may not want to be that drastic, but you can load up on the ones that work for you, and use them in different ways.

It's not unreasonable to have at least one card for each way that you use cards: one low-rate card for big, emergency purchases (like brake jobs and refrigerators) that you might have to pay off over several months; a small business card for your work expenses; cash-back cards that pay the biggest rewards for your gas, travel, and office expenses that you'll pay off monthly. And a zero-rate offer so you can burn some of your debt cost-free.

A Debit Card Is Not a Substitute for a Credit Card

In recent years, many consumers have begun using debit cards instead of credit cards for their everyday transactions. In fact, in 2006, the number of Americans using debit cards actually surpassed the number using credit cards. Lately there were more than 440 million debit cards in circulation in the United States.

But it's important to realize that debit cards are not credit cards. They may be convenient, but they don't offer most of the advantages of credit cards. In the first place, there's no credit involved. When you use a debit card, the money is instantly swept out of your checking account. So forget the float you enjoy when you use a credit card issuer's money for a month. Debit cards offer some rewards, but usually they are less generous than the rewards you can get on a good rewards credit card.

Then there's the big overdraft issue. If you miscalculate your checking account balance and use your debit card, even for a $3 cup of coffee or $1 pack of gum, you can be hit with typically egregious bank overdraft fees that are now averaging $34. And if you do that five times in one day, the bank can charge you five overdraft fees. I have heard from consumers who have been hit with hundreds of dollars in overdraft fees on a one-day shopping excursion without their bank ever denying the debits or notifying them that their account was overdrawn.

But here's the real reason I don't love debit cards: They're linked to your *checking* account. If your debit card is lost or stolen, you are liable for only $50 of losses when a thief uses your card to drain your account. And most banks will cover even that $50. But think about what happens in the meantime: The debit card thief goes on a spree with your card, wiping out your checking account. While you're waiting for the bank to fix the problem and replenish your account, the checks you wrote to your mortgage, credit card, and phone companies will bounce, creating a big mess and hurting your credit report and credit score along the way.

So use a debit card if you must—if you don't have a credit card, or if you can't trust yourself to pay off your everyday charges at the end of the month. But guard it carefully and consider it a stopgap measure: When you're at the point where you can use a good rewards card for your daily out-of-pocket expenses and then pay it off at the end of the month, put the debit card in a drawer and use *the* credit card instead.

All That Fine Print

But wait. Before you start applying for every credit card that's out there, you have to invest some time in studying the myriad ways in which the credit card companies will try to trick you into paying more and more in interest and fees.

If you feel like you're playing a game of "gotcha" with the credit card companies, you're not wrong. The banks that issue most credit cards have proven that they will do whatever they can to squeeze money out of us one way or another, and over the years a lot of people have gotten caught and really hurt by sneaky rate increases, killer late fees, hidden charges, and other outrageous and egregious practices of credit card issuers.

This is a relatively new phenomenon. Card companies used to depend on two sources of money for their income:

1. Fees that merchants pay to participate in card company programs so their customers can use credit cards (called interchange fees).
2. Interest payments from consumers.

But as interest rates have fallen in recent years, card issuers have scrambled to find new, different, and ever more painful ways to soak their customers. They've created fees and penalty interest rates for everything from paying your bill over the phone to being late on your electric bill. In 2003, banks made $10.7 billion in penalty fees; by 2008 that had almost doubled to $19 billion, according to R. K. Hammer.

Some consumers have gotten really beaten up by all of this and they have let their suffering be known. When the Federal Reserve started looking at how banks handle their credit cards and their credit card customers, it received 60,000 letters, almost all from angry consumers. That was more letters than it had ever received for a regulatory proposal.

Finally, late in 2008, the Federal Reserve and other bank regulators, including the Office of Thrift Supervision, which regulates savings associations and thrifts, and the National Credit Union Administration, which oversees credit unions, approved tough new rules to limit the practices seen as most abusive, such as the habit of the issuers to retroactively raise interest rates. But they delayed the effective date of those rules until July 2010, an 18-month delay that irked consumer groups and gave credit card issuers just the opening they needed to do whatever they wanted before the new rules kicked in.

Congress and the White House got involved, passing tough new legislation designed to curb the worst practices. This legislation goes into full effect in February 2010; until then it was open season on consumers. Card issuers jacked up their rates and fees as much as possible before the new rules kicked in.

New Legislation Kicks In

Many of the most egregious credit card practices will come to an end when the Credit Cardholders' Bill of Rights Act of 2009 goes into effect at the end of February 2010. It has these provisions:

- **Rate protections.** Issuers cannot retroactively raise interest rates on existing balances unless a customer's bill is more than 60 days past due. Issuers aren't allowed to raise rates on a customer simply because the customer is behind on payments to another lender, which is commonly known as the universal default clause.

(Continued)

Creditors can't increase the card's interest rate during the first 12 months after an account is opened, unless it is an introductory teaser rate, and these introductory rates have to last at least six months.

They must provide a 45-day notice of changes in rates.

If two or more different interest rates apply to different portions of an outstanding balance, the amount of any payment above the required minimum payment needs to be applied to the balance with the highest rate first and then to lower-rate balances. This is a huge change from the previous practice of most issuers. They typically offered a low, low interest rate on a balance transfer and a much higher rate on regular monthly charges. Then they applied all payments to the low-rate balance, so that you couldn't really pay off the regular monthly charges until the whole balance transfer was paid off.

- **Billing and payment protections.** They must provide a grace period for payments, even if the cardholder takes advantage of a promotional balance transfer offer.

   They can't use double-cycle billing anymore, meaning they can't charge interest for a balance that was paid in full the previous month.

- **Easier payments.** Card issuers must send credit card statements at least 21 days before the payment is due. They must accept phone and online payments without charging a fee for them (though they are able to charge a fee for expedited telephone and Web payments made on the due date or the day before).

- **Account management.** Creditors are required to post their written credit card agreements on the Internet. Consumers can reject credit cards that are issued to them without any notice of the card being added to their credit reports. This is important because often card issuers will offer consumers cards using language like "rates as low as" in their promotional material. It is only after consumers apply for the card that they may learn they don't qualify for the card they wanted, but instead were approved for a much more expensive card. The new law allows them to reject the card at that time, without it showing up on their credit reports.

   Issuers need to provide 30-day advance notice of closing an account.

- **Protection for young borrowers.** Issuers are no longer allowed to issue credit cards to consumers under age 18, unless they are emancipated or their parents are the legal cardholders.

   Anyone under the age of 21 who does not have any verifiable income no longer qualifies for credit cards unless their parents cosign the agreement, agreeing to be responsible for the debt.

What does this all mean? It means the card issuers are going to come up with a new bag of tricks and probably raise everyone's interest rate to the heavens.

People who pay their balances in full can expect to lose some of their benefits. Competition will keep rewards programs from disappearing altogether, but they will probably get less generous. Expect more cards to institute annual fees, shorten or even eliminate grace periods, and raise fees on balance transfers and late payments, two areas not addressed in the legislation.

The bottom line is you'll have to read your credit card statements and disclosures much more carefully. Banks and other issuers can be trusted to find creative new ways to make their money, so it's a little bit hard to predict where the new traps will be buried. Just trust me—they will be there. And here's one more warning to keep in mind: Business cards will be exempt from these rules, so all of those small business card solicitations you're starting to see? Caveat emptor.

The List of Shame

Here is a baker's dirty dozen of the bad card tricks that credit companies are still using, along with smart strategies for avoiding them. Some of them are ending thanks to that new legislation. I've included the current practices as well as how they are changing under the new rules.

1. Random rate hikes
2. Fees, fees, fees
3. Vanishing credit lines
4. Late payment traps
5. Convenience checks
6. Questionable payment allocations
7. Double-cycle billing
8. Universal default
9. Minimal minimums
10. A general lack of clarity
11. Bait and switch
12. Traps for travelers
13. Outlandish fees for secured cards

Random Rate Hikes

Card issuers can raise your rates because you're late on a payment, because you went over your credit limit, or because it's Tuesday and they just feel like it. And they have! My mailbox is replete with sad tales from people who were paying 3.99 percent one month and 21 percent the next.

Virtually all card companies retain the right to change the rates on their cards whenever they want to, and for whatever reason they choose, and they only have to give their cardholders a 15-day notice. Moreover, they can do it in a sneaky way: telling you that if you continue to use the card once they raise the rates, then you've "agreed" to the new rate for the balance you already carry. That's a retroactive rate increase! That's unconscionable!

Banks and other issuers have been having a field day with rate increases. Citibank and Capital One were among the first to jump in, raising rates across the board for many of their cards, even those held by customers who have always made timely payments. That was at a time when the cost of money to the banks was falling steadily.

As I write this, the federal funds rate (the amount banks pay to borrow short-term from the Federal Reserve and each other) is zero, and the prime rate is 3.25 percent. Banks are paying 1.4 percent on their short-term savings accounts and 2 percent on their certificates of deposit (CDs), according to Bankrate. And yet, the average credit card interest rate is 13.84 percent, reports IndexCreditCards. Sheesh.

> **The new rules:** Issuers are not able to raise interest rates retroactively on existing balances unless the cardholder is more than 60 days behind on payments.
>
> Rate hikes on future balances are not allowed until the card account has been open for at least a year and issuers have provided 45 days' notice.
>
> Issuers are allowed to raise rates, both retroactively and going forward, if it is the end of a promotional period or if the card is a variable-rate card and the increase reflects a normal adjustment of the rate because of an increase in its underlying index.
>
> **Winner's strategy:** Don't carry a balance, and if you do, watch your card's rates like a hawk. Call and complain if your rate

gets hiked, and if you can't convince your card issuers to reverse its rate hike, shop elsewhere for a lower-rate card. Consider shopping for new cards to compare rates.

Fees, Fees, Fees

You would think that card issuers would be happy with all of that interest income; in 2008, a year in which rates were falling and consumers were cutting back, they earned $101 billion in interest, according to an R. K. Hammer report. But, oh no. They've figured out that they can juice their earnings by charging fees for everything from paying your bill over the phone to taking cash advances to late payments. I have even seen reports of card companies charging $1 to customers who forget to enclose the remittance portion of their bill with their payment!

Penalty fees are charged for payments that are only a few hours late, and on transactions that put customers over their lending limit. (Shouldn't those transactions just be denied?) Late fees and penalty fees each run as high as $39, according to the latest survey by Consumer Action, a credit card watchdog group, which reports that the vast majority of issuers now charge both of these penalty fees—some as high as 3 percent of the outstanding balance.

Don't expect much improvement here. In fact, credit card issuers are widely expected to increase their fees as they lose interest income as the new rules go into effect. R. K. Hammer calls the shift to more fees in the future "undeniable." Look for a reappearance of the one fee that has mostly disappeared over the years: the annual fee. Many card companies will bring that back.

> **The new rules:** No over-the-limit fees may be charged unless the consumer has asked for the account to be set up to allow transactions that will exceed the credit limit. Even in those cases, only one over-the-limit fee may be imposed per billing cycle. Issuers aren't able to charge for online or phone payments, unless a service representative is involved.

> **Winner's strategy:** Follow the advice of Scott Bilker, who wrote *Talk Your Way Out of Credit Card Debt!* (Press One Pub., 2003). Never pay a fee without calling your credit card company to complain. There's an excellent chance you can get it reversed just by calling. That's the case with every

kind of fee companies charge, especially and including the annual fee. Stick with cards that carry no annual fees.

Vanishing Credit Lines

In 2008, bankers started doing something they hadn't done before: cut credit lines on good customers. Even people who were making their payments on time were finding their borrowing limits cut and their inactive accounts closed. In some cases, banks were penalizing customers whose credit scores had slipped; in other cases they were pulling back on credit simply because customers had items in their credit reports that bankers didn't like: Perhaps they lived in neighborhoods with high foreclosure rates or shopped at cheap thrift stores. American Express cut credit lines on one of every five credit card accounts it had.

This was all a response to the banks losing money on everything from bad mortgage loans to consumers not paying their credit card bills, as well as other questionable lending practices in the recent credit meltdown, and it's going to continue. Bank analyst Meredith Whitney has said that credit card issuers may pull back as much as $2 trillion in credit lines before the squeeze ends in 2010.

If you don't use your card to the max, this reduction in credit lines may seem like no big deal, but it has very troubling consequences for consumers. Even if everything else in your financial life stays the same, your credit score will fall if an issuer cancels a card or lowers your overall lending limit.

And some customers are hurt worse than others. Issuers have effectively frozen the accounts of some customers by lowering their credit lines to below the level of their outstanding balances. They can't charge anything new, and as they pay off their balance, the line drops to the new balance. This renders them creditless and also really damages their credit scores, which penalizes consumers who borrow to the max on their cards.

And—gotcha!—if you don't notice that your credit line has been cut back, you can incur an over-limit fee and penalty rate next time you try to use that card.

The new rules. Neither the new legislation nor the federal regulations attempt to limit an issuer's ability to cut credit limits.

Winner's strategy. Go back to Chapter 3 and do what you can to boost your credit score; this credit tightening will fall hardest on those who have lower scores. Keep more than one card, so that one issuer can't kill your credit. Do what Curtis Arnold, the founder of CardRatings.com, does to keep the cards he wants: He arranges to charge a recurring bill to each one automatically.

Late Payment Traps

It's remarkably easy to be late on your credit card bill, even if you're trying conscientiously not to be. That's because card issuers have worked really hard to trick you into paying late. They've cut the time between when they mail your bill and when your payment is due. They've arbitrarily set a time of day when your payment is due, and if your payment gets there, even 15 minutes late, it's "late." That's all so they can then slam you with those penalty fees and rates, of course.

The new rules: The new law tries to tackle those late payment traps. Card issuers are no longer able to set midday times when payments are due—they'll be due at 5 P.M. on the due date, and that due date will have to be the same date each month. It puts the onus on banks to mail their statements at least 21 days before the bill is due. That might create a whole other problem, though: The grace period is the time between when you incur a charge and when interest is first assessed on it. Typically, you have the first month of your statement to avoid any interest payments on new purchases if you aren't carrying a balance. However, existing Truth in Lending regulations require issuers to send notices 14 days before the grace period expires. It is conceivable that bankers will look at those two deadlines (14 days for the grace period; 21 days before the payment due date) and decide to end the grace period one week before the due date arrives. It is too soon to see how that will shake out. It's unlikely that banks will send two statements, but they could send one statement that has two due dates on it—one to avoid paying interest on new purchases, and a second to avoid late payment fees. Watch those statements carefully.

Winner's strategy: Late payment traps are actually among the easiest to avoid. You can authorize your credit card company to automatically take a minimum payment out of your checking account every month; that eliminates late payments and also leaves you free to send in additional payments as you'd like. Or, if you'd rather not trust your credit card company with your checking account number, you can authorize your checking account bank to electronically and automatically pay a more-than-minimum amount to your credit card bill every month, about five days before the due date. That will allow for due date shifts from one month to another.

Convenience Checks

They come in every bill, and in the middle of the month, too. They offer extra-low rates on cash advances and balance transfers. The rates can be as low as zero for several months, or under 3 percent for the life of the loan. Yeah, but—there's usually an up-front 3 percent transaction fee on these transactions. Until 2008, most of those transaction fees were capped at something like $60 or $75, making large transfers a good deal. Now, most of them are not, and you'll owe 3 percent to 5 percent on the total amount you transfer in the first month. Even if the rate you're getting after that is zero, that up-front payment means you're really paying the equivalent of a 5.5 percent rate for the year.

The new rules: There are no provisions relating to convenience checks.

Winner's strategy: Use these checks only if the rate is really great and it allows you to move debt from a more expensive card or loan. Try to find one that caps the transfer fee or eliminates it altogether. And don't use this card for anything else until that transfer is done, lest you fall into the next trap. Read on.

Questionable Payment Allocations

So, imagine you have a credit card with a zero balance. Its usual interest rate is 15 percent, but it offers a special 3.9 percent rate on convenience checks. You use one of those convenience checks to pay off a $10,000 debt. And then you used the card to buy $120 worth of groceries that month. Send in a payment of $120, and all of it will go toward paying interest and the $10,000 balance subject to the 3.9 percent balance. The $120 grocery debt will sit on your card and keep accumulating interest at 15 percent until the $10,000 has been paid off.

> **The new rules:** The new law's rules put an end to that practice. When different rates apply to different card balances, issuers have to either prorate your payments among all of your balances or apply all but the minimum to the highest-rate balance. That will teach them to prorate in a hurry!

> **Winner's strategy:** Make sure your various credit activities are segregated on different cards. If you're using one card for a low introductory rate or balance transfer offer, don't use the same card to charge regular monthly purchases.

Double-Cycle Billing

Double-cycle billing, also called two-cycle billing or dual-cycle billing, is a particularly egregious practice. It uses the average monthly balance over two months to calculate your interest, and has the effect of really slamming people who habitually pay off their balances but slip every once in a while. It ends up requiring you to pay interest in a month when you've paid your balance in full.

Here's how it works: Say that you pay off your balance in January, and then in February, you charge $2,000. Money is tight, so you make only the minimum $40 payment in February. In March, you charge nothing new, and receive a bill for $1,983—your balance minus the $40 payment plus a $23 finance charge. You pay it in full, and think you're done with your February cash flow problems. Not so fast! When the April bill arrives, it has an additional $11.50 in finance charges, because it's still using your (paid-off) balance to calculate your March interest due on your April bill.

> **The new rules:** Thanks to the feds, after July 2010, double-cycle billing will be illegal. But banks are squeezing what they can out of it before then.

> **Winner's strategy:** Find out before you use your card again whether your issuer employs double-cycle billing. If it

does, stop using the card, unless you're absolutely certain you'll always pay the balance in full. If you get hit with this anyway, call and complain. Specifically ask that the second month's interest be removed.

Universal Default

Some credit card issuers slap you with a punitive interest rate if you are late paying another card or unrelated bill, such as your phone bill. Consumers Union says it has even seen issuers raise rates on cardholders because they have opened another credit card or inquired about a car loan. That's outrageous, though the banks defend the practice, saying they have to protect themselves from customers who are becoming more risky.

> **The new rules:** The 2010 rules won't prohibit interest rate hikes based on these criteria, but it forces bankers to use the practice only on new balances, and only after the same 45-day notice that applies to other rate increases.
>
> **Winner's strategy:** Try the usual rate-increase tactics. Call and ask that the fee be lowered or use another lower-rate card instead. Do whatever it takes to pay off that balance quickly.

Minimal Minimums

Card companies only require you to pay a pittance when your bill is due every month. As you'll see, they want to keep it that way—the better for them to keep collecting interest on that debt forever. Their minimum payment usually is calculated as a percentage of your balance, typically 4 percent. Until regulators tightened the rules governing this in 2005, it was only about 2 percent of your balance. That was often not even enough to cover your monthly interest and fees.

Even at 4 or 5 percent, today's monthly minimums are inadequate, and will saddle you with debt forever if you think it's okay to "just pay the minimum." Want proof? Here's an example from the excellent calculator at www.bankrate.com/brm/calc/MinPayment.asp.

Say you owe $5,000 on your card and just want to pay it off; you're not charging anything new on it. The interest rate is a middling 14 percent. If you pay only the minimum ($200 the first month, $194 the next month, $189 the next month, etc.), it will take you more than 11 years and $2,003 in interest to wipe out that $5,000 balance.

> **The new rules:** The 2010 rules don't address monthly minimums, but some issuers are starting to raise minimum monthly payments on their own.
>
> **Winner's strategy:** When you get the bill and look at the minimum payment, say, "Ha! I laugh at the minimum payment." And pay as much as you possibly can. The savviest pay off the entire balance every month.

A General Lack of Clarity

If you didn't know all of this already, it's no surprise. Credit card statements and mailings are written to hide the dirty truth. In some cases, the envelopes carrying important disclosures are actually designed so that they look like junk mail and you will throw them away.

In 2000, credit card statements began including a table, often called a Schumer box (after card-company bloodhound Senator Charles E. Schumer, D-NY). It requires clear delineation of such items as the annual fee, the grace period, the annual percentage rate, and other effective interest rates, such as those on cash advances. But the Schumer box is still inadequate.

> **The new rules:** The new law requires these tables to include additional information in simple language in readable-size type about penalty rates and grace periods, and to offer other additional information. Issuers have to clearly disclose the period of time and total interest it will take to pay off a balance if only minimum monthly payments are made.
>
> **Winner's strategy:** Read everything your bank sends you, especially if it is in tiny type. If you're not sure about how your issuer is handling all of these issues, call and ask. If enough people call their credit card companies often enough, those

companies might decide to make their paper explanations a little more helpful.

Bait and Switch

It's not called bait and switch in the credit card world, but it's the same thing. You receive a solicitation for a great credit card and send in your application. The card you receive is worse: higher fees, lower benefits, higher rates. Why? The card company says that your credit score didn't fit the profile of the solicitation. Sadly, there's very little you can do to fight this.

> **The new rules:** The new rules don't stop bait and switch, but they can stop it from affecting your credit report. If you apply for one card but receive another, less valuable card, you can cancel it immediately without the card ever appearing in your credit file.

> **Winner's strategy:** Know your credit score before you apply for any new cards, even if the offer comes to you in the mail. Send back your application with a note, written right on the application, stating that you are applying for only the card that carries the terms mentioned in the solicitation and that if you are denied that card, you do not want any other card as a substitute. Does this always work? I'm sorry to say it doesn't. But it does sometimes work. Should you be given a card you don't want, cancel it immediately.

Traps for Travelers

Going abroad? Your card issuer certainly hopes so. Most charge a 3 percent transaction fee on all purchases made in another currency, on top of whatever spread they make with the actual currency conversion. That's 2 percent for the card issuer and 1 percent to kick back to Visa or MasterCard.

Not every bank has such hefty fees. You can find a handy chart with the latest at the IndexCreditCards web site, www.indexcredit cards.com/internationaltransactionfees/. Capital One doesn't charge any transaction fee on foreign transactions, though some reports say that its exchange rates may be less favorable. American

Express charges 2.7 percent. Some smaller community banks and credit unions may charge less.

> **The new rules:** Alas, there are no new protections for travelers in the new rules; in fact, more issuers seem to be increasing their fees for these transactions.

> **Winner's strategy:** It's still worth taking your card with you; most credit card issuers get a better exchange rate than you would standing in line at the airport or hotel kiosk. But before you go, try to line up a no-foreign-transaction-fee or low-fee card to take the trip with. And ask about the applicable exchange rate.

Outlandish Fees for Secured Cards

If you can only obtain a secured card because your credit profile is poor and you need to rebuild your credit, you'll have to pay $50 or more in fees. But the punishment should fit the crime and not be excessive. Some issuers ask applicants to pay fees that are higher than their total credit limit! So they'll deposit $200 for a $200 line of credit *and* have to pay the issuer $250 in nonrefundable fees. That should be against the law.

As the new rules go into effect in 2010, it will be.

> **The new rules:** The new law limits fees and security deposits to 25 percent of the credit limit when the account was opened, and additional amounts assessed in the first year would be held to 50 percent of the initial credit limit.

> **Winner's strategy:** If the only card you can get is a secured one, comparison shop to find one with comparatively low rates and fees. Make sure that the issuer reports your payment history to all three credit monitoring agencies, so you'll quickly improve your profile and move on to a better card.

And Now, On to the Good Stuff

Now that you've been warned about most of the trouble you can fall into with credit cards, here's the payoff: Steer clear of those traps and you can get more out of the credit card companies than they can get out of you.

You can use these techniques to squeeze your card issuers if you're disciplined about your spending and bill-paying habits, and if you have the cash flow to pay off your balances every month.

Here are my five favorite techniques.

1. Maximize your rewards.
2. Grab a free flight.
3. Get discounts.
4. Play the balance transfer game.
5. Use the float.

Maximize Your Rewards

There are some great rewards cards out there. One of my favorites is the American Express Costco True Earnings credit card. It's a cash-back card that offers rebates of 3 percent on gasoline, 3 percent on restaurants, 2 percent on airline tickets and other travel, and 1 percent on everything else, including those trips to Costco. Once a year, it gives you back your rebates in the form of a Costco credit. If you're a regular Costco customer, it's hard to beat this advantage.

Another popular rewards card is the American Express Blue Cash card. Credit expert Curtis Arnold, the founder of CardRatings.com, admits he is partial to this card. It has a tiered cash-rewards structure, so folks who don't spend much don't get great rewards. But once you've put $6,500 on the card, you get 5 percent cash back on everyday purchases like groceries and gasoline, and 1.5 percent back on everything else. If you spend a lot and learn to habitually charge everything, you can get a lot of money back on this card. The last time Curtis checked, he had gotten over $900 back in one year.

Here are my tips for making the most of those reward programs.

- Use these web sites to study the various rewards cards and programs out there:
  - CardRatings: www.cardratings.com
  - Index Credit Cards: www.indexcreditcards.com
  - Low Cards: http://lowcards.com
  - CardTrak: www.cardtrak.com
- Don't even think about it if you're going to carry balances. Rewards cards charge higher interest rates than other cards. A recent CardRatings.com survey found that the typical

cash-back card charged 14.54 percent a year whereas the nonrewards card average was 13.28 percent. If you're using a card for its rewards, pay it off every month.

- Use multiple cards so you can make the most of the rewards, but only if you're sure you won't lose track of all those bills every month. Many of the cash-back rewards programs cap the amount you can earn in a year at $300 or $400 or so. Learn those limits. If you spend enough to top them, keep separate rewards cards for each category of expense; for example, use one card that offers rich rewards on gas, another for groceries, another for home-improvement stores and the like. You'll get maximum rewards for each category, without topping out on any of your cash-back deals.
- Learn the rewards program rules. Some rewards expire if you don't claim them in a certain amount of time, so do what you must to make sure you collect your rewards. Some issuers require you to call and request them at $50 intervals; others just send them automatically.
- Go for the dollars, not the points. Many rewards cards offer points instead of dollars. These points can be traded in for gift cards and discounts at various retailers and their plans can seem enticing. But in these plans, a point is almost never worth any more than 1 cent on the dollar, the typical minimal cash rewards rate. So stick with the cash. It's less confusing and likely to yield a higher reward.

Grab a Free Flight

I'm not a huge fan of airline credit cards unless you travel all the time. Many of the airline cards carry stiff annual fees, and what's worse, they keep moving the goalposts on those free trips. Either it takes more rewards miles to get a trip, or they increase the blackout periods when you can't use the miles, or they allow only one or two seats per plane for frequent-flier mileage users.

But airline rewards can be a good deal if you travel all the time; you're already in the frequent-flier program of your choice, and you can use a mileage credit card to get your trips faster, or move yourself up to first class.

There's one other way to make the most of an airline card. Some of them now offer extremely generous sign-up bonuses: You can get enough bonus miles to cover a free trip as soon as you get the card and use it once. So, get the card, use it once, take the trip, and cancel. Duh!

Get Discounts

In an effort to build loyalty (and grab some kickbacks from retailers?), the big card issuers are all creating their own Internet shopping portals. Go to the web site of your credit card company, click through to its shopping program, and you'll be offered price cuts as high as 20 percent to shop at familiar retailers like Best Buy, Staples, and Home Depot.

These programs are all very similar, though each may list different retailers and different discounts for the same retailers. And you can get really bogged down searching from one to another, or window-shopping when you don't even need to buy anything. My advice? Register for every shopping portal your cards are associated with. If you're getting ready to make a sizable purchase, check your card issuer's site to see if it's offering a discount that day. Don't go overboard, or you'll waste time and money in unnecessary shopping.

Play the Balance Transfer Game

It is true that the balance transfer game is not as lucrative as it once was, but card companies are still offering zero-interest-for-a-year deals to new customers with top credit scores for a year or more. Use them!

If you're trying to pay off a high-interest debt on another credit card, or on a consumer loan or home equity line, apply for one of these cards. Try to find one that also eliminates (or caps) the 3 percent (or 5 percent) transaction fee for new customers. This may be negotiable; even if the offer doesn't say the fee will be capped, you can call and ask for it to be capped. Move as big a balance there as the card company will let you, and make sure you never make a late payment.

If this is the only consumer debt you have, try to pay it off before the promotional period is up. If you're making payments on other, costlier loans, just pay minimums on this zero-rate card until the year is about to be up. Then apply for another introductory offer on another card, and shift this balance over there. I know people who have done this with $30,000 at a time. Not only will you save big money on interest, but you'll also get the satisfaction of knowing you got a big bank to lend you money—for free!

Use the Float

Even if you don't have any big balances to transfer, you can still get credit card issuers to front you cash every month. Just carry your favorite card (or cards) with you and charge everything. No fuss, no muss, no running to the ATM machine or writing checks. (Remember those?) When you get your bill, pay it in full, on time. The advantage to you? Enormous convenience, and free float. To maximize your grace period, either remember or write down when each of your credit cards mails out its statement. Then charge on those cards when the statement most recently went out. For example, if a card bills you on the 5th of the month, use it most heavily from the 6th of the month on, and then switch your spending to the card that bills next in the month.

And that is why, despite all the tricks, traps, and troubles, I love credit cards.

How to Wipe Out Your Balances Once and for All

Remember the beginning of this chapter, where we talked about the two different worlds that credit card users inhabit? Now that we've surveyed the landscape, you can see how balance revolvers are at the mercy of banks, and those who pay off their cards get to turn the tables.

Now, you really want to pay off your balances once and for all, don't you? Here's all you need to know about that. In truth, paying off your balances is simple; there's nothing complicated about it. But it's not easy, because it does require sacrifice and scraping together the cash that will get it done.

- **Set your goal.** Make paying off your credit cards your top financial priority. Use the Federal Trade Commission's calculator (www.ftc.gov/creditcardcalculator) to see just how credit card interest drains your household budget. The average balance-carrying customer now owes $5,729 on his or her cards, according to the findings of a TransUnion survey.

Even at the comparatively low (for credit cards) interest rate of 14 percent, that's taking $67 a month in interest payments alone out of your budget.

- **Squeeze your budget.** Turn a cold eye toward your expenses and find some extra money to send to your credit cards every month. Do whatever it takes: cancel cable, eliminate dinners out, stop buying shoes, skip a summer vacation. Seriously. Once you burn this debt for good, you'll have even more extra cash for the niceties of life. But until you do, make this your priority.

- **Throw extra lump sums at the problem.** Tax refund? Check. Christmas present from Mom? Check. You can really jump-start your debt-paydown plan if you take drastic action. Hold a yard sale, moonlight as a babysitter or lawn mower, or do something at a higher earnings rate, if you have that option. Send all of your earnings to your credit cards.

- **Pay off the highest-rate card first.** That is, pay minimums on all of your cards, but send all of your extra payments to the card with the highest interest rate. Some credit card experts disagree with this advice, but they are wrong. They suggest that if you instead send extra money to the lowest-balance card, you'll burn that balance faster and it will make you feel better about the whole enterprise.

    You'll see why this advice is wrong once you look at the numbers. Here's an example from the excellent DebtSmart web site (www.debtsmart.com). Your Costly Card has an $8,000 balance at 19.8 percent interest and a minimum monthly payment of $160 a month. Your Bitsy Card has an interest rate of 5.9 percent, a balance of $6,000, and a $120 a month minimum. The two minimum payments equal $280, but you've figured you can pay an extra $120 beyond that every month.

    If you pay the extra $120 to Bitsy Card, you'll get it paid off in 27 months. At that point, you'll still have a balance of $7,068 on Costly Card. By the time you pay that off, at $400 a month, it will take you another 21 months, and you'll have paid a total of $5,120 in interest.

    Now go the other way. Pay only the monthly minimum of $120 on Bitsy Card, and pay $280 a month to Costly Card, the high-priced card. That balance will be burned in 39 months.

You'll be left with a $2,124 balance on the cheaper card, and it will take you less than six months to pay that off. Your interest total will be $3,740. At the end of the day, you'll have paid both cards off five months earlier, and you'll have paid $1,380 less in interest.

- **Use your HELOC.** If you're struggling under the weight of a high-priced credit card debt and you have a home equity line of credit on your house, you can consider using that line to pay off your credit card. The danger, of course, is that you'll run into trouble, lose your job, and not be able to make your payments. Then you could lose your house, instead of just your credit rating!

   So, don't take this step lightly. But HELOC rates are really low now; some are hovering just over 2 to 3 percent, and that interest is usually tax deductible. If you can easily afford the payments and have a secure source of income (and a backup source for a rainy day), you can take the credit card issuers off of your creditor list altogether by simply paying off your card with your home equity line. Then follow the same drastic-action techniques to kill that debt as soon as possible.

Accelerate Your Credit Card Debt

In the previous chapter, we showed you how you could burn your mortgage early using the mortgage accelerator strategy. Well, you can apply the same technique to burn your credit card balance more quickly than you might have thought possible. Of course, it is still better to pay off your balance in full every month, but if you find yourself with a balance you can't wipe out all at once, consider this technique.

Bill Westrom, the coauthor of this book, explains how to do this:

When you get paid, keep only the amount of money you absolutely need to write checks in your checking account. Send all of the rest immediately to your credit card as a payment against your balance. Then, all month long, use the credit card to pay for anything you would ordinarily pay for out of your checking account. So, use the card to pay your utility bills and your groceries; you've already sent the money into the card as a payment. Do the same thing with every subsequent paycheck. Along the way, remember to leave extra money in the credit card account as your actual payment.

This technique works because it reduces your average monthly balance and therefore cuts the amount of money you will have to pay in interest costs. And *that* allows more money to pay off your principal debt, faster and faster.

Here's an example: Say that you have a $5,000 balance on your credit card, and your interest rate is 13 percent. In that first month, you'll be assessed roughly $54 in interest; if you make the minimum payment of $200, your balance in the next month will only go down by $146, and you'll have a $4,854 balance.

Now imagine that you take home $4,000 a month. You leave $1,100 in your checking account to cover your mortgage check and cash needs and pay the remainder—$2,900—to your credit card company. All of the sudden, your balance declines to $2,100. As the month goes on, you use that card to pay for groceries, gas, and other expenses you have during the month. You consume and charge all but $200 of the amount you deposited into the card.

Your monthly interest falls to around $22, based on your new lower monthly average balance. (It will be slightly higher than this, depending on when in the month you spend the money by charging your expenses.) Out of your $200 payment, an additional $32 goes to paying down your principal. The following month, your balance is $4,822.

You can see how this can snowball in your favor. The reverse compounding effect will bring your credit card balance down much more quickly than if you simply sent in your $200 at the end of every month.

Of course, this technique requires serious discipline. Charge more than you send in every month, and you'll just be going backwards. Keep careful records of your payments and your bills to make sure you're accelerating your debt paydown, and not your troubles.

8

Car Deals: Making Sure You're in the Driver's Seat

Thanks to years of safety regulations, most cars aren't the "death traps" that Ralph Nader decried a generation ago. But they can still be death to your carefully constructed family finances if you don't know what you are doing. And it's very hard to know what you're doing, because most dealers would like you to stay in the dark—that's how they make the biggest profits!

The family automobile is probably the biggest purchase you'll make, other than your house and that college degree. And with most families owning more than one car at a time, and everyone buying a dozen or more over the course of their driving lives, it's safe to say you'll spend a lot of time and money on cars over the years. It's worth investing some of that time into learning how to get the best deal on the car and its financing—whether you buy or lease. It's one area where you'd expect consumers to hone their skills and do better with every new car they buy.

Yet the finances of automotive ownership have been moving in the wrong direction. Roughly half of all new car owners are underwater in their loans, meaning the cars they drive are worth less than the amount they still owe on them.

That's because of the convergence of a few anticonsumer trends: Cars got more expensive, and dealers got desperate. To keep those cars affordable, dealers got their finance companies to stretch out loans. The typical car loan is now five years long, and some go out as long as 84 months, or seven years—try holding on to the car that long and see how much it's worth! They also were letting consumers, including consumers with poor credit histories, drive cars off the lot with no money down. Not only was the dealer financing 100 percent of the car, but it was also financing sales taxes and extra fees. It's no wonder car financing went upside down and consumers slammed on the brakes. Sales of cars and light-duty trucks have fallen off a cliff, dropping about 40 percent from the previous year, and that was a weak year, too. That decline in demand has had an effect on used car prices, too, driving down the value of pre-owned cars and turning even more owners upside down.

That's where we are now. Many consumers are stuck with old, inefficient cars that they can't afford to sell. Some have car loans that they can't even afford to keep up. Others want a new car, but are afraid to negotiate with slick car dealers. Or they feel overwhelmed by the cascade of decisions that a new car involves: Foreign or domestic? Station wagon or minivan? New or used? Personal purchase or dealer? Hybrid or fuel-efficient? Lease or buy? Low-rate loan or cash back?

It is overwhelming, but there's also a lot of good automotive news out there now. There are tax rebates for people who buy electric or hybrid vehicles. (In 2009, Washington stimulated the automotive market with tax deductions and rebates for people who bought new cars, or who traded in old gas guzzlers for fuel-efficient ones. Those programs have expired, but it wouldn't surprise me if they were extended or reenacted.) In addition, car dealers have been heaping on incentives of their own, including price cuts and good financing deals.

Carbuyers can now access more competitive price data online than at any previous time. Later in this chapter I'll tell you where to get solid information about how much people are really paying for cars in your neighborhood. Having this kind of data before you go car shopping levels the playing field between you and the dealers. And those dealers are even hungrier than they were before.

I've spent a lot of time studying the car market for my work, so I can make the best decisions on my own cars. And I've talked to some of the most knowledgeable automotive insiders to get their take on how consumers can drive their own best deals. Here's the best of their advice, and mine, on how to profit from your next car purchase.

But First, Do You Really Need a Car?

For a minute, forget all of those incentives. There's nothing cheaper than delaying a car purchase for another year or two and living with the clunker you've already got. If your car is already paid off, you can spend a year or more tucking money into a savings account so you can put a hefty down payment on your next car. Or use that cash to improve your financial profile in other ways, by paying off credit card debt or other loans.

You can even delay car buying and do without a car if you don't have one or if you are sharing a car with your spouse or partner. You can embrace public transportation and use taxis or a car rental for the times when you really need a car. In some locations, you can use Zipcar (www.zipcar.com), an auto-sharing service that can be cheaper than a car rental.

How much can you save? If you are buying your car outright, the average car payment is now $484 a month, according to the National Automotive Dealers Association. (Lease payments can be lower, but often come with higher front-end and back-end fees.) Hold on to your car for one year longer and save that monthly payment. Even at a low 2 percent interest, you'll have $5,860 after one year, $30,500 if you can hang on for five. And you'll save money on insurance, too. So don't be in a hurry to get that new car. Nevertheless, the day will come when you're in the market for a new car. Here's how to proceed.

First, Figure Out How Much You Can Afford

Driving a car that you can't afford is the fastest way to get into trouble. In general, the full purchase price of your car shouldn't amount to more than 50 percent of your annual income, and your monthly car payment shouldn't exceed 12 percent of your monthly take-home pay. Add in all other costs (insurance, repair, gasoline, etc.), and it still shouldn't eat up any more than 20 percent of your monthly take-home pay, whether you buy or lease, according to Edmunds, the car research firm.

That means that you shouldn't consider just the sticker price of the car, but how much it costs to run. Some cars swill gasoline; others cost more to insure and still others have notoriously expensive mechanical problems. While you're comparing different car models, check the True Cost to Own calculator at Edmunds.com to see how much the car you're considering will actually cost to keep on the road annually. Choose a car that will fit your budget.

Decide Whether You Want to Buy New or Used

Many of my colleagues in the financial press are strongly in favor of buying used cars. They make the argument that new cars depreciate the minute you drive them off the lot and that buying a good used car means somebody else is taking the depreciation hit. Consider this advice from Liz Pulliam Weston, a financial writer at MSNBC:

> Buy used and drive it for at least 10 years. This one rule of thumb easily could save you tens of thousands of dollars over your lifetime compared with what you would pay buying cars new and owning them just five years. Not only will you buy half as many cars, but you'll avoid the 20% or so loss to depreciation that happens as soon as you drive a new car off the lot. Today's cars are better built and will last longer than ever before, so buying used isn't the gamble it used to be.

That may be true, but the same claim of longer-lasting, better-built cars can also be used to justify buying a brand-new car, especially if you prefer one that is inexpensive and fuel-efficient, and want to drive it for a long time. That's because those cars tend not to depreciate as quickly as flashier cars, and their owners don't sell them as often, either. So the price differential between a good-quality used car and a new car isn't as big as it once was. That 20 percent instant loss in value that Weston describes doesn't always materialize if you're shopping for practical cars like small Hondas or Toyotas. If you consider current dealer incentives and the better loan terms usually available on new cars, you may not save all that much by buying used.

You will, of course, save some money if you can find a good-quality used car, or if you are willing to drive a higher-mileage older car for a few years. Of course, you'll have to check it out carefully. You can get a vehicle history report from CarFax (carfax.com), which will give you detailed information about whether the car has ever been in a flood or accident. Many dealers will provide this report for free; CarFax charges $29.99. And have a trusted mechanic do a thorough diagnostic of the car, too. The American Automobile Association (AAA.com) lists qualified diagnostic centers on its web site, aaa.com.

The choices there are better than ever. New car dealers and used car specialists like CarMax usually offer warranties on their used cars, so you're not taking a big risk of the car falling apart on you as soon as you drive it off the lot. You can, of course, also deal person to person with the individual seller and find a good used car through a classified ad on Craigslist.com or in your local newspaper or car shopper. Just make sure that you have a mechanic check out the car before you do the deal. And check the vehicle identification number against the records at Carfax.com. You'll learn if the car's ever been in a bad accident or suffered flood damage.

Weigh the Hybrid Decision

Those 48 miles per gallon hybrids may have seemed tempting when gas prices topped $4 a gallon. But in fact, they may not really save you any money over conventional fuel-efficient cars.

That's because hybrids still cost a lot more to purchase, especially if you're talking about certain high-end cars. When Edmunds.com crunched numbers of hybrid cars versus the corresponding conventional cars, it found that some models would take so long to earn out as a hybrid that it wouldn't be worth it, even if gasoline was still priced at $4 a gallon. For example, it takes 18.5 years for someone buying a Toyota Highlander Hybrid to spend less than someone who buys a conventional Highlander. The posh Lexus LS600h Hybrid? You'd have to drive it for 84 years before it was more cost effective than its comparable conventional car.

Some hybrids are worth their extra price. The Prius and Camry hybrids paid off in under four years, Edmunds said. Finally, carbuyers can get federal tax credits for buying some specific hybrid models; find them at www.fueleconomy.gov.

And some people just feel better about driving a hybrid—they know they are contributing to a cleaner environment and helping to reduce the dependence on oil. Some consumers have perfect hybrid lifestyles. "If you are a person that keeps a car until the wheels fall off and drive a lot of miles, and you live in a city where there's a lot of stop-and-go traffic, you're a good candidate for a hybrid vehicle," says Jesse Toprak, Edmunds's hybrid expert.

You can do the math yourself. There's a nice little calculator called "Should You Trade in Your Gas Guzzler?" at http://political-calculations.blogspot.com. It allows you to consider all of the variables: how much you drive and where, how much you pay for gas, and how much it costs you to keep up the current car. It will give you a good idea of whether to go hybrid. There's another calculator at www.hybridcars.com/calculator/.

Shop Before You Shop

People who preshop online pay less for their cars than people who just walk into a showroom cold. If you're not sure what kind of car you want, study *Consumer Reports* and the Institute for Highway Safety crash test results, as well as recommendations from friends and neighbors. Narrow the choices down to two or three models, go out and test-drive them, and then come home and start researching prices.

There are now excellent web sites for finding out what people are paying for cars, so start at one of these spots:

- **TrueCar.com.** This new site offers current real data showing what people in your area are actually paying for their cars. It amasses data from dealers and tax and licensing authorities. It also has good data on what the dealers themselves are paying.
- **Edmunds.com.** The established leader uses dealer data to get what it calls "true market value" pricing.

Once you've gotten a good online estimate of what your car should cost, call or e-mail a few dealers and ask them to give you a quote for what they would charge for the car, bottom line, including all applicable fees and *not* counting incentives coming from the manufacturer. Have them submit their quote via e-mail, so you can print it out and take it in to the dealer.

Make the Most of Incentives

Before you drive to the dealer, go to the web site of the car's manufacturer, where you'll find the latest info on the kinds of incentives available for the car you are buying. Desperate carmakers are constantly offering an unprecedented, mind-boggling array of incentives.

Often you'll get a choice of either a zero percent interest rate loan or a cash rebate. There's no shortcut to making this decision: Use an online amortization or loan calculator to find out how much you'd pay in interest if you didn't take the cheap loan. If that's more than the rebate, go for the cheap loan. If it's less, take the rebate.

You may want to consider other factors, too. Often the zero percent financing deals are for shorter terms, like two or three years, and that might make the monthly payments unaffordably high. Some underwater car owners are using the rebates to pay off their old loans and purchase a new and more practical car.

You may decide to pass on the incentives altogether. After all, they aren't available on every car. It's not worth buying the car you don't want (or a more expensive car) just to get the rebate. You may do better than the incentives if you work with a buyer's agent. A good, independent buyer's agent will often be able to get you access to the incentives and a better bottom line price as well.

Should You Use a Buyer's Agent, Broker, or Buying Service?

The real luxury in the car market might not be the car at all, but the luxury of hiring someone else to do all of this work for you. Some people like the homework and the haggling; they consider it sport. Others would rather do anything else. If you're the latter, just hire someone else to handle the whole process for you. It's not as costly as you might think, and they will save you money and a great deal of time shopping for the car.

"You can never outsmart a dealer," says Linda Goldberg, a carbuyer's agent and one of my own most trusted sources of information about car deals. Her company, CARQ (www.carq.com, 1-800-517-2277), negotiates as many as 30 deals a month for consumers who are all over the country. They usually pay her $500 and save an average of $5,000, she says, because she knows the language of the deal. "I'm not working with retail sales; I'm working with owners and managers of dealers."

Goldberg spent 13 years in the automotive business doing sales, financing, and leasing before jumping to the consumer side. To find the best deal for her clients, Goldberg will shop a nationwide network of dealers. She once bought a car in California, had it shipped to her client in New Orleans, and still saved him over $1,000. She saved another client $10,000 off the suggested retail price of a car, and found $26,000 of hidden incentives for a Jaguar XK at a dealership right next door to where the client lived. As an independent buyer's agent, she receives only a fee and is bound to pass these incentives directly on to her clients.

Goldberg is one of very few buyer's agents in the car world. The typical agent works in a small, unglamorous office by themselves or with support staff. They are paid solely by the customers for whom they work. It's not an easy way to make a living and there aren't many of them. Goldberg reviews deals for car-buying clients in several different ways. Sometimes she simply reviews the deal they've already set and assures them they are getting a good price, or tells them they need to go back to the negotiating table with a specific lower price in mind.

In contrast, there are thousands of car brokers. Like brokers in the mortgage, stock, and real estate markets, car brokers are typically paid by the car dealers and not the consumers. That means they have a conflict of interest and may not get you the best, rock-bottom deal. You may not have to pay a broker $500, but you can be sure it will be built into the price you pay for the car. It's typical, says Goldberg, for a car broker to get a kickback of $1,000 to $1,500 for the car they sell, and that's money that's built into the price you pay. That can add $25 a month to your car payment. That being said, a broker can still help you find a car at a reasonable, albeit not rock-bottom price, if you'd rather not handle negotiations yourself.

Finally, there are big car-buying services, such as those run by Costco and the American Automobile Association. You can find several of them all together at Zag.com. Bottom line? They will leverage their buying power to get you a good deal, but it won't be a great, rock-bottom, awesome deal. They may get volume-based club prices for popular cars, but they don't negotiate individual cars and financing deals the way a dedicated agent would. Car buying services have little value.

Why Work with a Buyer's Agent?

Here's why I use CarQ and believe in using an agent or buying service:

- They know more than I do about the real costs and prices of cars.
- I don't want to deal with the dealers; it takes too much time and is too much trouble.
- They know where the financing traps are, and will avoid them.
- They will find a better total-cost/bottom-line deal than I would.

How to Pay for Your Car

The way that you pay for your car is as important to your family finances as are the decisions you make about when to buy a car and what car to buy. Your choices are:

- **A traditional car loan.** Auto loans are actually pretty competitive right now. Recently, the average interest rate on new car loans at auto finance companies hit an all-time low of 3.17 percent, according to the Federal Reserve. Of course, that figure includes all of the zero percent incentive rates that are prevalent now. You may, however, have to give up the best price on the car if you take the promotional interest rate deal.
- **A car lease.** Leasing a car typically offers you a lower monthly payment than a car loan, though of course you won't own anything after the (typically three-year) lease expires. Leases can be a particularly good deal for people who deduct some of their car costs as a business expense, or for drivers who like to get a new car every three years.
- **A home equity loan.** Remember the HELOCs we discussed in the last two chapters? This could be the best way of financing your car. You can bring a check to the dealer and negotiate the best price on the car, because you aren't using dealer financing. HELOCs typically offer lower rates than car loans. And the interest is likely to be deductible.
- **Other alternatives.** There are even people who are successful in paying for their cars with their credit cards. It sounds crazy, but if you've got a good credit score and can grab one of those 1.99 percent for the life of the balance offers, you can put the car on the credit card. If you do that, reread the credit card chapter to make sure you avoid the hidden pitfalls that you can fall into with that strategy. Don't use that card for any other purpose until you've paid off the car.
- **Cash.** Of course, the very best way to pay for a car is cash that you've saved up for just this purpose; you'll pay nothing in interest! Once you've paid off your current car loan, keep making those payments to your savings account until you are ready for your next car. The more you can put into a down payment, the lower your payments and interest costs will be.

Getting the Best Loan

At least a month before you go car shopping, check your credit scores, as I described in Chapter 3. Do what you can to raise your scores, and then start loan shopping *before* you start talking to car dealers. Both Capital One (http://capitaloneautofinance.com) and E-Loan (www.eloan.com) are known for offering competitive rates on auto loans. If you're a member of a credit union, you should certainly check there first. The most recent data from the Credit Union National Association (CUNA) shows that credit unions tend to charge 1.6 percentage points less than banks on new car loans; consumers who get their car loans through credit unions save an average of $1,000 over five years, says CUNA's economist, Mike Schenk.

Once you have those quotes in hand, you'll know exactly what numbers your dealer will have to beat. If you can get a good low rate on a private loan, it gives you more leeway to negotiate on the car's price with the dealer.

Try to keep the length of your loan to five years, or even less, if you can swing the monthly payments. That way you won't get locked into owning a car too long, or end up with the same upside down problem so many hapless owners are now facing. If you have to go out seven years to afford the car of your choice, seriously consider choosing another car altogether.

Fixing the Loan You've Got

Did you know that you can refinance a car loan, just as you can refinance a mortgage loan? This little-known option is especially worthwhile for one group of borrowers: those folks who had to settle for a bad loan because they had a bad credit score when they bought their car. If you've been making your payments in a timely fashion for a year or more, it's worth checking to see if your score has improved enough to qualify you for a better loan. Look at the lenders mentioned in the previous section and find others online by searching for "auto refinance." If you still owe $15,000 on your car, and have three years left on a 12 percent loan (not unusually high for poor-scoring borrowers), you can save $37 a month, or $1,332 over three years, by dropping down to a 7 percent rate.

The Leasing Alternative

To tell you the truth, I almost always lease my own cars. That's because I fit the profile of a person who should be leasing: I like to drive a new car and I don't drive a lot of miles. It's my philosophy that you should buy assets that appreciate and lease assets that depreciate, and almost nothing depreciates as fast as a brand-new car being driven off the lot.

And right now, there are some very favorable lease deals on the market, especially from foreign manufacturers, and especially on more expensive cars. If you lease a car, you can also save on the state sales tax, because you pay tax on only your monthly lease costs and not the whole car. Linda Goldberg of CarQ recently ran a comparison for me, just to demonstrate how a moderate-priced car kept for three years could save you money on a four-year lease. Assuming a $20,000 car driven 12,000 miles a year and a 5 percent interest rate, it works out like this: The lease payments are $243.28 a month and the car payments if you purchase are $503.16 a month. After four years, you'll have paid a total of $11,677 for the car lease, but you'll have paid $24,152 to own the car. The owner would have to sell it for $12,475 or more, or drive it that much longer, to break even with the person who leased it.

Of course, the person who leased the car would be faced with having to find another car after those four years. You'll almost always spend more over the long term by leasing a car than you will by buying a car and driving it past the point where it's paid off. That's what we usually do with my wife's cars. As a family, we lease one fairly new car, and I get to drive that one to local appointments. (Thanks, honey!) Our second car is a paid-off workhorse that my wife uses for errands and that we use for longer trips. We drive that one into the ground.

So, should you buy or lease? As the lease-peddlers like to say, you can get twice as much car for the same monthly payment if you lease instead of buy, but that's only if you expect to get a new car every three or four years. You may do better with a lease if you put fewer than 15,000 miles a year on your car and if you expect to sell or trade in your car in three or four years. That may describe you even if you aren't all about new cars. For example, what if your kids are teens and you just want a minivan for their high school carpool years? Leasing also works very well for self-employed people who need to use their car in business and can deduct their monthly car expenses from their taxable income.

Of course, the lease versus buy question is another that can best be answered with a calculator. Here are a few:

- www.leaseguide.com/leasevsbuy.htm
- www.dinkytown.net/java/BuyvsLease.html
- www.edmunds.com/calculators/auto_lease_calculator_index .html

If you've decided you'd rather lease, you still have a lot of homework ahead of you. There are more variables with a car lease deal than there are with a car purchase, so you have more points to negotiate and worry about as you put your deal together.

In general, I think it's a good idea to negotiate the price of the car first, as if you were buying the car. Once you've done that, work out the rest of the lease issues. There are many of them, and they are complex, so I'd like to make two points about that. First, it's a good idea to go into the lease negotiations with a worksheet that includes all of the different factors. You can find a good one online at www .leaseguide.com, and another at www.wheelsdirect2u.com.

Second, you should know all the different line items that go into a lease calculation, but you may not be able to negotiate exactly what you want on all of them. The important strategy, then, is to consider the whole package and choose the lease that gets you the best bottom line at the end of the lease. Even after you've figured out what the car's purchase price should be, you should get more than one lease offer from different dealers before choosing the best one.

- **Lease length.** Three years is usually where the sweet spot is, in terms of low payments and a car that's still what you want it to be. Most manufacturers will now guarantee a car's service for three years, so you won't be faced with the problem of having to spend money fixing a car that you're about to return. Adding three extra months, going out to 39 months, makes the monthly payments lower and is usually what I do.
- **Residual value.** That's the amount the car is expected to be worth at the end of the lease. If you decide you want to buy the car at the end of the lease, this is the amount you'll pay for it.

Negotiating this number is tricky; the lower it is, the better it is for you at the end of the lease, but the higher the lease payments will be. If you're relatively sure you don't want the car after the lease is over, a higher residual value can be a better deal for you.

- **Open-end or closed-end lease?** If you sign an open-end lease, you are taking all the risk that the car will be worth less than the residual value at the end of the lease. You'd have to pay the difference, even if you didn't buy the car. Dealers like open-end leases because they protect the dealers from the risk that the car will sharply decline in value while you are driving it, so open-end leases can cost less in monthly payments than closed-end leases. But they are a bigger risk for consumers, who typically opt for closed-end leases, where the residual value is locked in and you can walk away at the end of the lease. Almost all leases now are closed-end leases; it's unusual to find or sign for an open-end lease.

- **Mileage.** What's a standard amount that you will be allowed to put on the car? This is typically 15,000 miles. If you go over this amount, you may have to pay an extra amount per mile when you turn the car in. Some dealers will try to limit annual mileage to 10,000 or 11,000 miles, and Mercedes has just started working with a 7,500 mile limit for people who don't do a lot of driving. It lowers the driver's cost, and Mercedes gets a decent, low-mileage car back that it can resell.

- **Capitalized cost reduction.** This is a fancy term for up-front money; it's the lease equivalent of a down payment. Subtract this amount from the price you negotiated for the car, and what you're left with is called the acquisition fee, or the capitalized cost of the car to be leased. You should always pay the "cap cost" up front. It is considered part of the purchase price of the car, and will be subject to sales tax. Don't roll extra fees into the lease's CCR, or they will become subject to taxes, too.

- **The money factor.** This is the number in the lease that will be used to calculate your monthly payments. It isn't the interest rate, but it corresponds directly to the interest rate. You can usually calculate the implicit interest rate by multiplying the money factor by 2,400. For example, a typical money factor now might be 0.00208. Multiply that by 2,400, and you'd get an interest rate of 5 percent.

- **Maintenance and insurance requirements.** You'll be responsible for taking care of the car and insuring it, just as if you owned it. Make sure the lease clearly states your requirements, the specific standards for normal wear and tear that the dealer will accept when you turn the car back in, and the terms of the warranties.
- **Additional fees.** Your state may levy other licensing fees; the dealer may try to build in additional lease fees. Get a full accounting.

The Other End of the Deal

When the lease is over, you'll have the chance to buy the car at the residual value or to walk away. Usually, it is best to walk away. If you want to change your mind and your car before then, good luck! Most leases don't allow you to end the deal early or renegotiate. You may be able to find another driver to take over your lease at LeaseTrader. com, but it will cost you possibly as much as a month's lease payment to post and transfer your lease.

So, take the time to be sure before you lease—or buy—a car. And that's probably the best last word on the subject. It takes a while to get all the little details right when you're doing a car deal, so don't rush into it. If you need a car in a hurry, perhaps because yours got totaled in an accident, consider doing a short-term rental while you slowly and deliberately find your best deal on wheels.

CHAPTER 9

An Education in College Costs

There's a lot of craziness about the whole college scene, and I'm not talking about frat parties. I'm talking about staggering tuition bills, shuttered lenders, and a student loan infrastructure that has gotten so big, burdensome, and out of whack that it literally ruins some people's lives.

That's sort of a paradox, because the truth is that college is one of the few expenses in life that it is really worth going into debt for. You've probably seen the statistics: A college degree is likely to be worth almost $1 million over a lifetime of earnings, according to a study done by the U.S. Commerce Department's Census Bureau. That number goes up with every additional degree: Those with master's degrees earn $400,000 more than college graduates over their earnings years. Those with PhDs earn $1.3 million more, and a professional degree such as a medical or law degree is worth roughly $2.2 million more than a bachelor's degree over the long haul.

And college-educated people tend to be healthier and happier over their entire lives than those who stop their formal education after high school. So yes, that degree *is* an appreciating asset and well worth obtaining, even if you have to borrow money to do so.

But not too much money, and not in the wrong way. Tuition costs have risen at rates greater than inflation for 45 of the past 50 years, making college less and less affordable. (In the 2008–2009 school year, public colleges and universities raised their tuitions 6.4 percent on average, and private schools raised theirs 5.9 percent, according to the College Board. Consumer inflation, in the 12 months leading up to those announcements, was only 2.6 percent.) Some of the priciest private schools now charge more than $50,000 a year for tuition, room, board, and fees. Yikes!

Affordable forms of student aid, like government-subsidized loans and grants, failed to grow as quickly as those tuition bills. Banks and other private lenders saw that gap as an opportunity to profit and rushed in. In 2007, the student loan industry erupted in controversy, when Andrew Cuomo, New York State's attorney general, investigated the industry and found ethical lapses. Some schools were steering students to lenders that had kicked money back to those same schools, or in the worst cases, to the administrators themselves.

Just as schools and lenders started cleaning up those ethical problems, the credit crisis hit. Many college lending companies exited the market altogether as the loans became less profitable. At the same time, the meltdown in the stock and bond markets slashed college endowments, and the recession squeezed state treasuries. Schools raised their tuition rates and fees to make up for their lower revenue streams, but cash-strapped families seemed less able than ever to pay the higher cost. The gaps between what colleges charge and what families can pay has continued to widen.

Some of that may change as President Obama's education policies and budgets start to filter through the system. He has proposed that the federal government take over the student loan business through the Department of Education. Instead of guaranteeing loans from private lenders, the Department of Education would make all of the government-supported loans itself. He has also proposed that Washington put more money into grants for the neediest students.

But even if his plans become law, money for college will remain tight, and schools are likely to continue "gapping" kids—giving them less aid than their family needs to meet the school's total cost. Government-guaranteed loans may become more costly as interest rates rise, and middle-class families will continue to find themselves squeezed the most, with too much income to qualify for the best financial aid but not enough to comfortably pay for college.

Every family has to figure out how to navigate all of this for themselves, because there are myriad ways to approach the college funding decision. There are some great strategies and tools for paying for college, even if you're already a high school senior.

And there are some smart new strategies and products for paying off college loans you may already have.

The best way to approach paying for college is by thinking of it on a time line. The solutions and strategies that work when you're saving for your new baby won't work if you wait until junior is 15 and taller than you are. Here's a step-by-step approach to making sure your family has the money for college when you need it—without letting student loans squash your child's dream career or future.

Baby Steps: Save, Save, Save

There's nothing better than having the money in hand when it's time to matriculate. If you've got the cash, you don't have to worry about the financial aid morass, and your child can choose the school she wants on the basis of other factors. He or she may even stand a better chance of getting in if the school knows that you won't be asking for aid.

So, start early. If you set up an account when your baby is still a baby, you can feed it with every birthday and family event. You can get grandparents and uncles and aunts into the act, too. If you can squeeze $250 a month into your child's account, and earn an average of 5.5 percent a year on it, by the time he's 18, he'll have $82,726 to spend on college.

Years ago, the best way to save for a child was by putting the money in the child's name. Parents saved taxes on the income that the money earned, because kids' tax rates were typically lower than their parents'. But tax policies changed, and now kids must pay income taxes on investment income at their parents' rates until they graduate from college or turn 24, whichever comes first.

Now, there are new ways to pay for college. Over the past few years, Congress has created and institutionalized two tax-favored forms of college savings: the Coverdell Education Savings Account and the 529 college savings account. I'll tell you about them in a minute, but first, here's a heads-up warning about both of them: Key provisions of both accounts will expire in 2010, and Washington will have to do something to keep them operating after that. Most experts believe Congress will act before the deadline—who wants to be the guy who stops people from saving for college? But that's not set in stone, as they say, and these provisions could change after this year.

Coverdell Education Savings Account

The Coverdell Education Savings Account is the best first way to save for college if your income isn't too high to qualify. In 2009, you had to make less than $110,000 a year in adjusted gross income ($220,000 for joint filers) to qualify; that limit will rise with inflation in 2010.

These alternative accounts, also called Education IRAs, allow you to set aside as much as $2,000 a year for each child. The money earned in the account is tax free if it is withdrawn to pay for college. You can set up your own Coverdell account at many mutual fund companies, banks, and brokers, and make all of the investing decisions yourself. That $2,000 may not seem like much, but consider this: If you put $2,000 into an account earning 5 percent for your daughter on the day she is born, and add $2,000 every year on her birthday, she'll have more than $61,000 for college by the time she turns 18.

State-Sponsored 529 College Savings Plans

State 529 plans allow you to stash far more money, and offer better breaks if you are in a high tax bracket, but they are problematic. There are no income limits, and some states allow you to put as much as $350,000 into a 529 plan—over time or all at once. Some states also offer tax deductions for some portion of your contributions. And the money the account earns is not taxed if you use it to pay for college. You don't have to use the money within the state, or for any state-sponsored school.

But these plans have their problems. Each state runs its own plan, usually with management from private financial companies, so you can't choose your own money management firm. Many took very big risks in stocks and nonguaranteed bonds in the past few years, and families whose kids were just a few years away from college lost a lot of money in them. That wasn't supposed to happen. Finally, some of them have very high fees. These problems can be so significant that Greg Brown, an analyst with Morningstar, Inc., a Chicago research firm, has called them "fundamentally flawed." His advice? Use a 529 plan if you make a lot of money and have a lot of money available to save. And don't just choose the plan your state offers; compare plans to see which one gives you the best combination of low fees and good investment choices. You can compare plans at these web sites:

- **Saving for College:** A clearinghouse of information about all aspects of saving for higher education (www.savingforcollege.com).
- **College Savings Plans Network:** A site sponsored by the states that offer college plans (www.collegesavings.org).
- **Morningstar:** This research firm analyzes the best and worst 529 plans every year (www.morningstar.com).

How to Fix Your 529 Plan

What if you already have a 529 plan (or several, one for each child), and have lost a lot of money in it over the past two years? Here are a few strategies you can follow:

Close the account and take the loss. You can close a 529 plan in which you have a loss and deduct your losses, but the rules for doing this are complicated. Instead of being a capital loss, the loss is counted as a miscellaneous deduction, so you only get to deduct your loss to the extent that it exceeds 2 percent of your adjusted gross income. And this could trigger the alternative minimum tax, so check with your tax pro first.

Switch plans. You can move money from one state plan to another once a year without penalty. If you suspect the plan you're in is lousy, shop for a better plan and transfer the money. Even if you have to give up your own state's tax deductions to get a better plan, that might be worthwhile.

Shift beneficiaries. If you have more than one child and the oldest one's 529 has had big losses, consider finding another means of paying for the first child's college and saving the 529 plan for a younger sibling.

Wait. You can pay the first year or two of your child's college through other means and give the 529 plan time to recover some of its losses. Or save it until your child goes to graduate school. Most states do allow their plans to be used for that.

Save and invest for yourself. Finally, if you're underwhelmed by the 529 choices out there, and either have maxed out on a Coverdell or make too much to qualify, consider just investing in your own name for your child. If you set up a mutual fund or brokerage account and feed it regularly, you can use the money for college when it's needed, or save it for other family priorities if it isn't.

You can sell losing investments and use those losses to offset gains. You can let that money continue to grow while your child is in school, and have your child take college loans. When he's done with college, you can give him the shares, and he can sell them and pay taxes at his (presumably lower) tax rate. Then he can use the proceeds to pay off the loans.

You can also limit taxes in that account by using it to invest in tax-free municipal bonds and bond funds.

Saving money without using any specially designated account does give you a lot of flexibility. Just make sure you don't put the account in your child's name. There's no tax advantage to that, and it could hurt his ability to get financial aid. Or get blown on his tattoo and piercings hobby as soon as he turns 18.

High School: Learn How the Financial Aid Game Works

There are steps you can take when your child is in junior high and high school to prepare her for getting the most possible financial aid. Of course, she should be preparing for this by getting good grades and participating in after-school activities, so that colleges will want to pay her to attend. The more you know about how financial aid works, the more ready for it you will be.

Here are the basics: When your child is a high school senior applying for colleges, you'll be filing out the financial aid applications. State schools will use a federal formula and private schools will use their own private formulas for determining how much you and your child can afford to pay. This is called your expected family contribution (EFC). Each college will then, individually, figure out how much it costs to attend for a year, subtract your EFC, and then make up the difference with a package of federally guaranteed loans, grants (that are free money), and on-campus jobs for your child. Many schools now leave a gap between their price and the EFC for the family to fill with more expensive private loans. They tend to do this strategically, "gapping" the students they are only lukewarm about and not gapping those they really want.

That means there are two ways for your family to increase the aid your son or daughter will get: Make them more desirable to the school, and lower your expected family contribution.

The EFC weighs a number of factors, including your earnings and your savings, and the amount of money in the child's name. It also considers your age on the theory that older parents need to keep more of their savings for their own retirements, whereas younger parents can afford to pay out more for college.

The best way to figure out how your family's EFC will stack up is to run your family numbers through an online EFC calculator. One of the best is at the FinAid web site at www.finaid.org. This is probably the most authoritative independent web site about financial aid.

You'll learn that having high taxable income counts against your child's ability to get aid, and that having savings also counts against you, though having debts doesn't help. Put that all together and you will learn some good strategies for positioning your child to apply for aid in her senior year. Here's how:

- Sell winning stocks and mutual funds by December 31 of a child's junior year of high school. That way those gains won't show up in your taxable income in the year, starting January 1 of his junior year, that the colleges look at.
- Pay off debts with assets. Don't keep a high-interest car loan and $25,000 in the bank if you think your child will qualify for aid. Pay off the loan and get that $25,000 out of your bank account.
- Shift earnings, if you have that ability, out of the child's junior/ senior year and into earlier or later years; so take your annual bonus in December of his junior year and in January of his senior year, for example.
- Move money out of your child's name. If your child has a sizable nest egg, spend it on him while he's in high school, and replace it with savings in your name. Use it for summer camp and his cell phone, for example, and deposit a like amount into your account. Student money often counts more heavily in the EFC than does the parents' money.
- Start hunting for scholarships. There are thousands of private scholarships available for students, some with big money and some aimed at very special targets, such as bassoon players, residents of specific counties, or people with certain names. Some scholarships are aimed at members of particular religious groups, or those aspiring to specific careers. The more

narrowly focused the scholarship, the more likely you are to get it. The bigger awards are more difficult to get. But it's one way (another is a part-time job) that students can contribute to their own education. You can find out all about scholarships and apply for them at FastWeb (www.fastweb.com).

Senior Year of High School: Tough Decisions

Early in your child's senior year, you should establish at least a rough idea of how much you can afford to pay for college. This doesn't mean you shouldn't apply for high-priced schools; many of them have the most money to give away. But it will give you all an idea of what the family's bottom line is.

In January of the senior year, start applying for financial aid by filing out the Free Application for Federal Student Aid (FAFSA) form, available from the U.S. Department of Education at www.fafsa.ed.gov. You must also fill out the PROFILE form, created by the College Board, for private schools, and available at the College Board's web site (www.collegeboard.org). The schools on your child's target list might have additional financial aid forms of their own.

By April 1, all of the schools will let your child know whether he was accepted. At the same time, the schools will send a financial aid offer to your student.

And this is when you have to analyze the amount of debt built into that package and make some tough decisions about loans.

What about Those Loans?

Students coming out of school with big debts are facing up to the realities that they can't afford to go to graduate school, or choose low-paying public service careers, or stay home with their children, all because they are struggling with student loans. The advocacy organization Project on Student Debt has collected some of their stories. There are folks like Kevin, who owes $66,000 between undergraduate and graduate school and faces $500-a-month payments for the next 20 years. Or Lisa, who is unemployed and married to a teacher. She and her husband owe $127,000! They will be trying to scrape together cash for their kids' college funds before they finish paying for their own.

So, minimize those loans, especially if your child isn't sure of what he wants to do after college. To do that, consider alternative ways of saving money on the cost of college. Perhaps your child can squeeze four years into three, or work full-time and go to school part-time. Or take a year off between high school and college, to start earning money for school. Or start at a less expensive school or community college, do well, and then transfer to the pricier alternative for the last two years and the big-name diploma. There are options besides simply signing on the dotted line that the financial aid office will give you. Got that? Good. Now, it's time to decide about those loans.

The financial aid package your child receives may include some grants and some work-study opportunities, but the bulk of the package is likely to be made up of loans. Here are the varieties you might encounter, and what to do about them.

Stafford Loans

These are the most common loans and can come directly from the U.S. Department of Education (called direct loans) or from private lenders receiving government guarantees (called a Federal Family Education Loan, or FFEL). Students with financial need qualify for subsidized loans; other students are offered unsubsidized loans. Some are offered a combination of both.

Unsubsidized Stafford loans have a fixed interest rate of 6.8 percent. Subsidized rates for the school year that starts in the fall of 2010 are 4.5 percent. They are slated to go to 3.4 percent in the following year. Interest is charged on Stafford loans from the moment the money is disbursed; the government pays the interest on the subsidized loans until the student leaves college.

The federal government limits the amount of Stafford loans any student can get, as follows:

- Freshman year: $5,500. No more than $3,500 of this amount can be in subsidized loans.
- Sophomore year: $6,500. No more than $4,500 of this amount can be in subsidized loans.
- Junior and senior year: $7,500 each year. No more than $5,500 of this amount can be in subsidized loans.

Students who are independent of their parents—or whose parents fail to qualify for government-sponsored loans—can borrow an additional $20,000 over the four years.

> **The smart strategy:** Stafford loans are not bad, if you will need to borrow money for college. Rates are low when compared to other unsecured debt. They come with a variety of repayment options that can give you flexibility once you graduate and start paying them back. But they are loans, so you should consider other alternatives, which I'll get to shortly. If you have another way to come up with this money, you are free to take the rest of the financial aid package and not take the loans.
>
> And you can also comparison shop for Stafford loans. Even though they all charge the same interest rate, some lenders offer discounts during the repayment period for automatic repayments and making timely payments. You can check other offers at Simple Tuition (www.simpletuition.com) or Bankrate (www.bankrate.com) to see if there's a better deal than the one your college aid officer is showing you. Your college has to process loans from other lenders, even if they aren't on the college's preferred list.
>
> Finally, it's a good idea to try to pay the interest on the loan while your child is still in college. The federal government will pay interest on the subsidized loans while she is in college, but if your child takes any unsubsidized Stafford loans, you can pay the interest yourself while she is in school. That will keep it from compounding on itself. And that interest may be tax deductible, too.

Perkins Loans

These are government loans aimed at the neediest students and awarded through the colleges. As Mark Kantrowitz of FinAid likes to say, "the Perkins loan is the best student loan available." Because it is subsidized, the rates are a low 5 percent. Unlike Stafford loans, interest won't begin to compound until nine months after graduation, and Perkins loans offer more opportunities for graduates to cancel their loans by going into public service jobs.

The smart strategy: If you must borrow for college and qualify for the Perkins loan, take it.

The PLUS Program

The Department of Education subsidizes a gap-filling program for parents that is called the Parent Loan for Undergraduate Student (PLUS) loan program. It is available to any parent regardless of income. These loans are also made either directly from the Department of Education or privately through the FFEL program. Parents with reasonable (not subprime) credit scores can qualify for PLUS loans that will completely fill the gap between the cost of college and the financial aid package. They aren't cheap—PLUS loans charge 8.5 percent interest from the day the money is disbursed. And up to 4 percent in fees charged by the government and the private lenders is tacked on as well.

The smart strategy: Legislation passed in 2008 allows parents to defer PLUS loan payments until six months after the student has finished school, but don't do that. Start paying as soon as you take the loan to keep the interest from snowballing on you. Consider other alternatives before you take a PLUS. And do comparison shop. PLUS lenders also offer discounts for various repayment options, such as making payments through automatic drafts from your checking account. You can find a comprehensive list of lenders and their discount offerings at Mark Kantrowitz's FinAid site. You'll have to fill out a separate credit application at the college financial aid office to get a PLUS loan.

Private Loans

After the government-sponsored aid is exhausted, there's another category of loans you will hear about from your financial aid office. Private education loans are simply loans from banks and other lending companies that are used for college costs. They are like car loans, but without the collateral of the car, and usually have variable interest rates. They are loans to students who rarely have credit histories, so the rates can be astronomically high—18 percent or more. Parents are usually asked to cosign the loans, which can bring the rates down to prime plus 0.5 percentage points. You can get private loans through your school or through your bank, or through a number of other lenders (however, some lenders have left the market, claiming these loans aren't profitable).

> **The smart strategy:** Avoid private loans if possible. If you feel you must—say your child was accepted into a very competitive program that will allow him to graduate immediately into a great job, and your whole family thinks it's worth it—then do cosign the loans, to keep the interest rates within reason. Comparison shop carefully, because there is a wide variety of products available in this category. Don't be swayed by the name of the loan; some are branded with college names or titled to sound like government programs, but they are simply private loans. You should also check in with your credit union. Many offer college loans that are cheaper than the bank loans.
>
> If you do get private loans, choose programs that let you start repaying them immediately, so that you're not amassing additional interest on top of interest. For example, Sallie Mae has a new Smart Option private loan program that allows the students to pay the interest on their loans while they are in school. (Of course this often involves the parent paying the student to pay the interest.) But that is worth doing; it keeps the interest from compounding to astronomical levels, and it helps the student build a good credit score.
>
> Private loans are also sometimes called alternative loans, but they aren't the true alternatives I have in mind when I think of that word.

Alternatives from Your Own Life

When I think of alternatives to financial aid, I don't think of pricey private loans. I think of other ways your family can raise the money. One place to look is your house. If you have substantial equity in your house, you can consider getting a second mortgage, refinancing your home to pull cash out, or using your home equity line of credit (HELOC) to pay some of those college bills. This is a good source of cash, far better than taking on an expensive private loan. The interest on the HELOC is likely to be tax deductible, and the rates are lower because it is secured debt. Of course, don't put your house at risk for more than you can afford to pay, but consider this a reasonable alternative if you've got the equity and the means to repay the loans.

Then there are intrafamily loans. Perhaps grandparents have investments but need income. They can lend money to the college child or pay the tuition directly to the college, and you can repay them every month. Set up correctly, this can be a win-win situation; you can pay higher interest than your parents will probably earn elsewhere, and it will still be less than a bank loan. To do this, set it up right; you can set up a simple contract, or use a web site that will administer the loans for you. One company that does this is Virgin Money, at www.virginmoneyus.com.

There are also new peer-to-peer lending sites that you may choose to use. These sites put together people who need money with people who have money to lend and want to earn interest. The rates available on this site may beat those offered by banks, especially if you have a good credit score.

Leading peer-to-peer lending sites include:

- Prosper, www.prosper.com
- Fynanz, which specializes in student lending, www.fynanz.com
- Lending Club, www.lendingclub.com
- Loanio, www.loanio.com
- GreenNote, www.greennote.com

Finally, there's good old-fashioned belt tightening. This is different for every family. I just spoke to one father of a Harvard undergrad who said, "We are mowing our own lawn and cleaning our own house for the next four years." A single mother I know, who is scrimping to put her daughter through New York University, has rented out her daughter's room for the four years she is in college. That may seem extreme, but on graduation day both mother and daughter will be happy they minimized the loans.

Credit Cards

You'll notice that I haven't mentioned credit cards as a source of college money, even though as many as 30 percent of college students are paying tuition on their credit cards, according to college lending company Sallie

(Continued)

Mae. More than nine of every 10 college students use credit cards for textbooks, school supplies, or other education expenses.

Like other credit card use, this has two sides to it. Surely, some families are charging tuition for the convenience and the credit card rebates, and paying off their bills with savings. But too many students are charging themselves into trouble.

The average college student graduates with credit card debt over $4,100, says Sallie Mae, and most students are surprised at the size of their bills when they receive them.

So—don't use credit cards for college, unless you're one of those credit-card winners who is only doing it to juggle card rewards or make the most of those last few zero percent interest offers. Do encourage your kids to use *one* credit card in college for convenience, but make them receive and pay the bills themselves out of their own spending allowance. Parents who simply get the bills mailed to themselves and pay them while their child is in college aren't doing the kids any favors, and they aren't teaching them anything.

After College: The Bills Come Due

Six months after you graduate (or withdraw from school without the diploma—a big mistake if you've got loans), your first payment is likely to become due on the loans.

Whatever else you do, do this: Pay your bills on time. Your payment history will be reported to the credit bureaus. And most lenders offer some rate reductions after you've made timely payments for a period of three years or so. Most lenders will also give you a discount if you agree to have your monthly payment drawn automatically from your checking account.

Students can consolidate all of their government-backed loans into one big loan, but the decision should be made carefully, as I'll explain. Consolidation loans simply average the interest rate on all of the loans to come up with the rate for the new loan, so there isn't an interest rate advantage to consolidating.

But consolidation does allow for a greater variety of payoff options: Consolidation loans can sometimes stretch your payback period for as long as 25 years, greatly lowering your monthly payment (but increasing the total amount of interest you will pay). With a consolidation loan, you can also get a graduated repayment plan, so that you make bigger payments in later years, when you presumably have a bigger salary. You may also be able to get an income-contingent repayment plan (from the Department of Education) or income-sensitive repayment plan (from private lenders), which adjusts your monthly payment annually, based on how much you are making. The whole consolidation loan business is in upheaval, with most private lenders having declared the business unprofitable and stopped making these loans. The Department of Education has picked up the slack. If you think you want to stretch out your repayments, you may find consolidation worthwhile. Here are my guidelines:

- **Do consolidate PLUS loans.** There's a loophole on all of the federal student loan regulations that can save you a little bit of money if you've taken out PLUS loans. Mark Kantrowitz, publisher of the authoritative FinAid web site (www.finaid .org), explains it thus: The federal rules cap the interest rate on consolidation loans at 8.25 percent. But the current rate on PLUS loans is 8.5 percent. Consolidate them, and voilà! You've cut 0.25 percent interest off your debt. On a $25,000, 10-year loan, that only cuts $3 and change out of your monthly payment of $310. That's not huge. But you could take yourself out for popcorn and a movie on your savings every few months.
- **Don't consolidate if you have a lot of Perkins loans.** Their longer grace period and other advantages can be lost if you roll them up with your Stafford loans.
- **Consolidate Stafford loans.** This won't save you any money, but it won't cost you anything, either. And it's easier to have one bill a month than half a dozen. You'll buy yourself more leeway in paying the loans back, and if you stretch out their repayment you can use your cash flow for other items like a house down payment or a career wardrobe. You can always pay extra as your career builds to pay those loans down more quickly, if the interest rates stop seeming low in comparison to rates you could get elsewhere.
- **Consolidate private loans, maybe.** Consolidating private student loans is just like refinancing a car loan: Maybe it's a better deal, and maybe it isn't. Be sure to check with lenders to see if

they are willing to roll several of your private loans into one, and what the new rate and other terms will be. If the interest rate is better, go for it!

New Options from Uncle Sam

In recent years, Washington has approved a few new programs to ease debt burdens on college graduates. See if one of these works for you.

- **Income-based repayment plan.** This program is aimed at people who want to work in low-paying fields, or who run into medical or other problems that keep them from working. It enables them to consolidate their government-subsidized loans into a more affordable loan. The income-based plan caps monthly payments at 15 percent of your monthly discretionary income, and defines discretionary income as the difference between your adjusted gross income and 150 percent of the federal poverty line. (The 2009 annual poverty threshold for a single person was $10,830; 150 percent of that is $16,245.) If, for example, your adjusted gross income as a schoolteacher is $35,000 a year, your monthly payments would be capped at $235. If your earnings are low enough, your monthly payment could go to zero. If, after 25 years, you still haven't repaid your loans, they will be forgiven. You don't have to consolidate to get on an income-based repayment plan. You can find out how to get an income-based repayment plan at a special site set up by the Project on Student Debt at www.ibrinfo.org.
- **State teachers loan forgiveness programs.** Looking for a career as a teacher? Many states and municipalities offer student loan payoff programs for their educators. They vary by state in terms of which types of loans are eligible and how the repayment plans work. But storm clouds are gathering: In the past couple of years, Kentucky, Iowa, Pennsylvania, and New Hampshire have cut back on these programs. If you're getting ready to commit to a teaching program in the hope that it will repay your loans, check the state treasury and political climate first!
- **Public service loan forgiveness program.** Anyone aiming for a government or nonprofit career should consider consolidating

directly with the Department of Education and stretching their payments as long as possible, so they can qualify for this new program. It will forgive any student debt remaining after 10 years, as long as you're still employed in that field. There are many details, also available at the same IBRinfo web site. But it's nice to see a new plan that really aims to help the helpers!

CHAPTER

10

Don't Let Bad Luck
Derail Your Finances

Troubles happen, especially in troubling times like these. Jobs disappear and they take their health insurance benefits with them. People get sick. Homes—and whole neighborhoods—lose their value. Bills pile up and good people get buried under them. One misstep or bit of bad luck and it can all fall apart.

That's not a statement about you; it's just life. If there's a silver lining to the recession, it is this: If you've got trouble, you're in good company. So many people have been slammed. There's no shame in losing your job, or finding yourself stuck in a bad mortgage, or facing a pile of medical bills you can't handle. The *New York Times* recently ran a long personal article by its own economics correspondent, Edmund Andrews, in which he described how divorce, job loss, and treacherous mortgage products had put his family into debt hell and foreclosure—and he's an economics expert who earns more than $100,000 a year!

For a lot of reasons, our credit system has stopped working for average Americans. But here's what's even worse: There are some people and businesses out there that are just waiting to take advantage of your bad luck and make things worse. They may have fraudulent products to sell—like debt settlement plans that don't really work. They may be collection agents who call you all day and night, threatening to ruin your credit or poison your reputation at work. They may be bankers who cut your credit limits just as you need cash the most or raise your monthly payments beyond your ability to stay even.

They've even created new ways to get you in trouble. People who have jobs, earn money, and pay their bills on time are now getting trapped by new credit industry practices. This actually happened to Christopher Viale, a friend of mine who runs one of the best credit counseling agencies there is—Cambridge Credit Counseling Corporation. Chris knows exactly how credit works, and he earns a decent salary and pays all of his bills on time. But this is what happened to him: He used low-rate credit cards to charge about $100,000 in home improvement expenses when he was building a handicap-accessible home for his special-needs family. All was well; he and his wife were comfortably making all of their payments and expecting to pay off their debt over time. But his credit card issuer, Bank of America, cut his credit lines down to the level he had already borrowed, which lowered his credit score. Once his score fell, Bank of America then raised the interest rates on his BofA cards from an average of 5 percent all the way up to 26 percent. Suddenly, Chris's monthly minimum payments more than doubled—up to $1,700 a month. Any extra money that he had been paying to work down his balance was now going just to keeping up with the interest.

Knowing what he knows about how the credit card issuers work, Chris was able to fight back: He was able to get Bank of America to restore his lower interest rates.

He fought back, and you can fight back, too. With the right moves, you can contain financial troubles so they don't infect every other aspect of your life. You can tap into the new programs and the great resources that are out there to help you—and stay away from the bad guys. You can save your house—and your future. You can get the health care you need at a price you can afford, and beat back the debt. You can get to a place where you are in control of your money instead of the other way around. And you can come through your troubles stronger, better, and more financially fit.

That's what this chapter is for. Regardless of how you find yourself in trouble, I am here to help. I've gathered the best of the new programs, along with the solid and trustworthy strategies I've discovered over decades of work in the personal finance field. Read on for specific strategic advice if you find yourself in any of the following situations.

- You're over your head in credit card debt.
- You can't keep up with your mortgage.
- You don't have health insurance.

- You're being hounded by debt collectors.
- You have medical problems and big medical bills.
- You've lost your job, or think you may be about to.
- You aren't making ends meet.
- You're making all of your payments, but you feel like you're barely hanging on, and have no resources for emergencies.

Doing Debt Triage: How Much Trouble Are You In?

You already have a good idea about whether you need a financial fix. Perhaps you've done the self-assessment exercises in Chapter 2, or perhaps your sleepless nights are telling you something. But you may not know how bad your problems are. There are roughly three levels of debt problems, each with its own solution.

1. **You may be able to dig out all by yourself.** If you're able to make more than minimum payments on all of your bills and your credit score is good, you may be able to fix your own debt problems.
2. **You may need a credit counseling agency to help you.** If you can't make all of your monthly minimum payments, and your debt is rising every month instead of falling, you may be able to dig out with the help of a credit counseling agency. They can help you budget so you can make higher payments toward your debt, negotiate lower rates with your creditors, and put you on a debt management plan (DMP) that will set an affordable schedule for paying off your debts.
3. **Bankruptcy may be your only or best option.** If you're so underwater that you don't think you could pay off your consumer debts in three to five years, even at lower interest rates and with a debt management plan, you may be a candidate for bankruptcy. A good credit counseling agency will tell you when to contact an attorney. I'll deal with that in the next chapter, but let me just say this about that subject: There is life after bankruptcy. In the current environment, walking away or rescheduling your debts in bankruptcy court may be the best possible solution for some people.

Prioritizing Your Bills

If you temporarily don't have enough money to pay all of your bills, you might have to skip or delay payments while you figure out how to get out of your debt problems. But make sure you don't skip bills that would have what my colleague Liz Pulliam Weston, author of *Deal with Your Debt* (Pearson Education, 2006), calls "catastrophic consequences" if you don't pay them.

That puts your mortgage on top of the list, in my book. Falling behind on your mortgage hurts your credit report and score quickly and for a long time; at worst you can lose your house for not paying your mortgage. (If your mortgage *is* the problem, go back to Chapter 5 for advice about new programs to help consumers with mortgage problems.) Your home will be protected—even through bankruptcy—if you stay current on your mortgage.

Look at the list of all of your monthly bills, and decide which ones must be paid and which ones you could let slide for a little while. Here's my approach, in the order I think you should make sure your bills are paid.

1. Your mortgage, or, if you're renting, your rent.
2. Other home loans, including your home equity line of credit (HELOC) and any second mortgages you might have. You can make the minimum payment on your HELOC.
3. Car payments and auto insurance, especially if you need the car to get to work. It will be repossessed if you fall too far behind, and your late payments will be reported to the credit bureaus.
4. Health insurance. A health emergency added to a financial setback is a catastrophe. Keep your coverage.
5. Credit cards—make minimum payments.
6. Utility bills. You usually have a few months' leeway before somebody turns out your lights or shuts off your water. One missed month won't affect you very much.
7. Lawyer, doctor, and dentist bills. You don't want to stiff your professionals, but they are not likely to turn your bill over to a collection agency or notify the credit bureaus until many months have passed. In many cases, they are also willing to show forbearance if you call and describe your situation.
8. Personal loans from family and friends.

Finding Cash: Desperate Times, Desperate Measures

Many times, you can dig your own way out of troubles without calling in outside help. If you have a solid credit score, you may be able to create what businesses call a debt restructuring plan. That is, move debts around to lower the interest rates and the payments on your outstanding debts. For example, that would include shifting credit card balances to lower-rate cards.

These are the steps in a do-it-yourself get-out-of-debt plan:

1. List all of your debts, their interest rates, and their minimum monthly payments.
2. Make the required minimum payments on all of them every month.
3. Send any extra money you can come up with to the debt that has the highest interest rate.
4. Once you do away with that balance, send that payment, along with extra cash, to the next-highest-rate debt.

You can jump-start your own debt repayment plan by raising a bit of extra cash in a hurry: Hold a yard sale, scour the house for items you can sell on eBay, or take a second job evenings or weekends. Sell your second family car. These moves may not seem worth the bother, but gaining even an additional $500 at the beginning of your debt repayment plan can cut years and hundreds of dollars off your payments. Putting that $500 toward a credit card charging 18 percent interest will save you seven years and $350 in interest.

So, find some cheaper sources of money to burn those high-rate debts. Here are some places to look.

- **Low-rate cards.** If your credit score is solid, you may be able to use balance transfer offers to shift those balances to cards offering lower interest rates. That will help you pay them down faster. There are traps here, though, so reread Chapter 7 to learn the right way to do this.
- **A home equity line of credit.** Should you use a home equity line of credit to pay off other debts, like credit card debts? Often that's a good idea. The interest you pay on your home equity line of credit is usually deductible. The rates are far lower than credit card rates. You can use your home equity line of credit to pay off all of your credit cards and other high-interest loans, and then use the mortgage acceleration techniques I laid out in Chapter 6 to get it paid down fast.

  But there are two reasons why you may not want to do this:

1. You may prefer to keep your home equity line unused, in case you want to tap it for future emergencies.
2. You will be putting your house on the line for debts that are now unsecured. Be absolutely, positively sure that you will be able to pay the home equity line off before you take on that extra risk.

- **Personal loans from friends and relatives.** If you're paying 18 percent on your credit cards and your parents are earning 2 percent on their savings, there's a place in the middle where you'll both profit from a personal loan. But don't do this if you're in danger of default—the last thing you want to do is take Mom's retirement down with you. It's a good idea, if you take a personal loan, to structure it in a formal way. You can write a contract that includes an interest rate and a payment schedule. If you want help, you can get it from Virgin Money, a company started by Richard Branson, who also founded Virgin Airways. It will calculate interest, create a contract, and arrange automatic payments so that the whole arrangement can go forward smoothly. Find it at www.virginmoneyus.com.

- **Peer-to-peer lending.** Want to take a chance on borrowing from a stranger who isn't a bank? The Internet has made that possible. Several web sites exist to put people with money to lend together with people who need the money.

  The market leader is Prosper, at www.prosper.com. It will screen your request by pulling your credit report and score and making sure you are likely to repay the loan. Then it will allow you to post your loan request on the web site, along with your story. The rates you pay will be higher than a low-cost credit card or home equity line, but lower than a high-rate card. Other peer-to-peer lending sites include Lending Club (www.lendingclub.com) and Loanio (www.loanio.com).

- **A collateralized bank loan.** Do you have some savings? You can offer to deposit them in a certificate of deposit at a bank or credit union and then borrow against them. Not all banks and credit unions will do this, but some will, at rates that are better than your credit card rates.

- **Your own 401(k) plan.** Typically, advisers say it is a bad idea to borrow from your own retirement plan, because it reduces the ability of your retirement plan to compound; but it isn't always a bad idea. Here's why: The interest you pay on your 401(k) loan is interest you pay to yourself. It gets deposited into your account. And while the interest rate, typically prime plus one percentage point, is lower than what your account may earn invested in mutual funds, it is also lower than the rate you'll pay on most of these other emergency sources of cash. You also don't have to qualify for a 401(k) loan based on your credit score, and you can get the money quickly, usually within about a week of applying for it. If your employer allows it, you can borrow money from your 401(k) plan (usually up to $50,000), pay off your credit card debt, and repay your own retirement fund with monthly payments.

Working with Creditors

You may also want to contact your creditors directly to see whether you can get them to help you pay them. You stand a particularly good chance of getting some concessions if you can demonstrate that you want to repay your debts and you have some special reasons, such as disability, unemployment, or surprise costs, such as roof repairs and tax assessments, that kept you from making your regular payments. *Don't* let them talk you into putting the balance on a credit card or signing a new loan to cover the bill. That's the opposite of a concession; it's a bigger headache for you.

There are good strategies for negotiating with creditors, and one of my favorite sources for specific advice in this area is Nolo Press. This is a California legal self-help firm that publishes legal documents, forms, and letters that consumers can use to contact creditors and work out debt solutions. If you have a lot of debts and want to work them out yourself, it's worth investing in Nolo's credit repair book, by Robin Leonard and John Lamb. This book comes with a useful CD. (You can find it listed, along with other resources, at the back of this book.)

Individual creditors, such as dentists and home improvement contractors, may be the easiest to negotiate with. They may agree to payment plans that will allow you to stretch out what you owe without piling on interest.

Do not contact your credit card company until it's clear that you will not be able to restructure or pay your debts. Credit card issuers talk a good game (and even set up a web site called Help with My Credit at www.helpwithmycredit.org) to steer troubled borrowers to the right resources. But, in truth, calling your card company may hurt you more than it helps. Once your issuer knows you're in trouble, it might cut your credit limit and raise your interest rates, or even close your account. All of that can lower your credit score and accelerate the rate at which your troubles mount.

However, once you're at the point of not being able to make minimum payments on your bills, though, you should contact your credit issuer. Ask to speak to a supervisor. You can request that the issuer reverse certain charges, like over-limit fees or late fees. You can ask for a lower interest rate, or try to work out a repayment plan. You may not get far, but at this point it doesn't hurt to ask.

Warning! Don't Go to a Debt Settlement Company

They have different kinds of names, usually with words like "Relief" or "Solutions" or "Freedom" featured prominently, and they typically promise to make your creditors settle for pennies on the dollar of your debts. But what they all too often do is pile hefty fees on top of your existing debts while they fall short of their promises. They try to sell you the moon, but they don't deliver anything.

"These companies prey on people who are doing the right thing by seeking to manage their debt and get control of their finances," Andrew Cuomo, New York's attorney general, said recently. "With all of the problems we face in this time of economic distress, it is outrageous that these firms are targeting those who are the most financially vulnerable." New York is one of several states that are investigating the debt settlement industry, which has burgeoned in the past decade.

A debt settlement company is typically a for-profit company that promises "debt relief" without details. They are *not* the same as credit counseling agencies. They may say they'll collect your money and negotiate concessions from your creditors. Most creditors pledge not to cooperate with them. They may simply be selling you a new, more expensive consolidation loan (also not a good idea).

Not every debt settlement firm is a fraudulent one, but even the ones that may be run legally are expensive and don't deliver solid results. Often, your penalties and interest pile up on top of the big debt-settlement fees and you end up in worse shape than when you started.

My advice? Just stay away. I recommend credit counseling instead.

Student Loan Troubles

There are special provisions for people who can't afford to pay off their government-backed student loans. It's important to contact your lender before you stop paying your bills; many of the student loan solutions are available only if you are not already in default on the loan. Here are some of your options:

- You may be able to get your loan deferred; your lender may agree to temporarily delay assessing interest or sending bills if you're back in school, unable to find work, or suffering another economic hardship.
- You may get other concessions, even if you can't get a deferment. Your lender may offer to reduce or skip your payments, though interest will continue to accrue.
- You can consolidate your loans to get a better payoff schedule. Reread Chapter 9 to see how to consolidate your loans. But know that a new government program allows you to consolidate into an income-based repayment plan that will lower your monthly payments to a level you can afford on your salary, even if it's a low salary. These plans will allow you to skip your payments altogether if you're not earning any money. Find more details at www.ibrinfo.org.
- You can get the U.S. Department of Education to help you. The department has a special ombudsman office simply to help people with student loan problems. Contact this office at (877) 557-2575 or e-mail fsaombudsmanoffice@ed.gov.

Call-In Credit Counseling

If you've done all that you can on your own and you still feel buried in debt, you should definitely seek credit counseling. A solid, reputable credit counseling agency can help you assess your situation and offer advice on how you can work your way out of debt. It can also put you on a debt management plan (DMP) that will get your creditors off your back and get your debts all paid off in a reasonable amount of time.

But there are also some real limits to how much they can help. And not every credit counseling agency is a good one. I'll give you some recommendations and good, solid tips on how to get the most out of a credit counseling service, but first a little bit of historical perspective is in order.

The credit counseling industry was born in the mid-1960s, mainly with support of the creditors who wanted to be able to collect debts that had gone bad. They paid fees to the agencies, most of which were nonprofit, and the agencies were able to use that money, called "fair share" funding, to set up business. They would counsel consumers, get concessions from the lenders, and create debt management plans for consumers. When consumers were enrolled in a debt management plan, they would have a set amount to pay every month and they would have a set date when their debts would be paid off. Credit card issuers would often cut their interest rates—sometimes to as low as zero—to make the debt management plan work. The consumer would pay nothing, or minimal amounts, for this service. So far, so good, but the industry was about to take a turn for the worse.

Travis Plunkett, the legislative director of the Consumer Federation of America, has spent the better part of his career monitoring these agencies, and has testified extensively before Congress on problems in credit counseling. He says the problems started when, over the years, creditors started paying less to the agencies and they needed to go to consumers to earn money. The legitimate not-for-profit agencies got squeezed, because they were getting less in fair share fees. A new breed of aggressive for-profit credit counseling agencies came on the scene and made their money by leaning on consumers.

By the late 1990s, credit counseling had gone seriously off track. For-profit companies (and some nonprofit agencies with close ties to for-profit companies) began aggressively marketing DMPs to people who didn't need them. They charged high fees. Consumers began complaining to the feds. Congress finally stepped in in 2006 with a new set of standards for nonprofit credit counseling agencies. These require agencies to counsel consumers even if they are unable to pay and don't want a debt management plan. They also require that by 2011 nonprofit credit counseling agencies receive no more than 50 percent of their revenues in fair share fees, to limit the influence that creditors might have on their advice.

At the same time, the Federal Trade Commission (FTC), the Internal Revenue Service, and the Justice Department all started issuing standards or examining credit counselors.

As a result, the industry is far cleaner than it was before 2006, even strong consumerists like Plunkett agree. But are they more helpful?

Only within limitations. Creditors have gotten tougher with consumers in debt management plans, so the leeway you'll get from your card company once you enroll in credit counseling isn't as broad as it once was. "It is becoming increasingly clear that the DMP is a less viable tool in helping consumers significantly reduce their unsecured debt, because creditors have kept interest rates too high," says Plunkett. The Consumer Federation of America surveyed card issuers in 2009 and found that many had raised the rates they'd assign to accounts in DMPs. All were charging more than 5 percent, with Capital One charging 15.9 percent and Discover charging a range of rates as high as 15.9 percent.

Of course, with some troubled consumers facing rates as high as 29 percent on their accounts, even those rates might be helpful for some. And there are signs that issuers are starting to realize that they are better off lowering their rates and getting paid through a DMP than they are squeezing their customers into bankruptcy filings, so credit counselors are starting to get some additional concessions.

Bottom line? Yes, by all means, call in a credit counseling agency if you can't manage your debts by yourself. In fact, contact two or three before deciding which one you want to work with. A good agency will get you concessions from the card companies that you won't be able to get by yourself. And it will offer solid budget counseling, too.

How to Choose a Credit Counseling Agency

Credit counseling agencies can be in your neighborhood or across the country, but not every area has a credit counseling agency. Some of the best work via phone and e-mail with clients all over the country.

I do have a favorite. I like Cambridge Credit Counseling, a national firm headquartered in Agawam, Massachusetts (www.cambridgecredit.org or 800-897-2200). This is a company that had pre-2006 problems, but now is a cleaned-up nonprofit with a new management and board of directors. Here's what I like about it: Cambridge is well funded and can afford to spend a lot of time on counseling and budgeting services. They also help you restore your credit after you have been on the program for a while by writing you reference letters and vouching for you with potential lenders. It's not just about shoveling out debt management plans.

But it isn't the only agency in the book. There are three other solid places to look for credit counseling.

- **The Justice Department.** Bankruptcy law now requires consumers to get credit counseling before filing for bankruptcy, so the Justice Department has vetted and published a list of counseling agencies it says are qualified to perform prebankruptcy counseling. They are all nonprofit, and they are all run legally. You can find the list by doing an Internet search for the words "trustee credit counseling" or at this web site: www.usdoj.gov/ust/eo/bapcpa/ccde/cc_approved.htm.
- **National Foundation for Credit Counseling.** These agencies were the first national nonprofits. You can find a local counselor through their web site at www.nfcc.org or by calling (800) 388-2227.
- **Association of Independent Consumer Credit Counseling Agencies.** This industry association does include some for-profit companies, but it also has standards of conduct for all of its members. You can find a counselor through its web site at www.aiccca.org or by dialing (866) 703-8787.

The FTC recommends that you ask these eight questions before working with an agency:

1. **What services do you offer?** Look for an agency that offers more than just debt management plans. It should have a range of budget counseling, savings, and debt management classes. They should discuss your entire financial situation and help you come up with a long-term and ongoing money management plan. If having a face-to-face meeting with your own counselor is important to you, make sure you find a local agency that offers those sessions.
2. **Are you licensed to offer your services in my state?** Not all states require counseling agencies to be licensed, but if yours does, you should make sure the firm is licensed.
3. **Do you offer free information?** A good agency offers educational materials without charge.

4. **Will I have a formal written agreement or contract with you?** Even if you choose to work with a national, Internet-based agency, you should have a formal agreement. And should you go ahead with a debt management plan, you should get it all in writing and read it carefully before agreeing to participate.

5. **What are the qualifications of your counselors?** Try to use an organization whose counselors are trained by an outside organization that is not affiliated with creditors.

6. **Have other consumers been satisfied with the service that they received?** You can check the agency with your state's consumer protection office and the Better Business Bureau to make sure there aren't complaints about it.

7. **What are your fees?** Are there setup and/or monthly fees? A good nonprofit generally offers free budget counseling. It's typical to charge a setup fee of $50 or less, and monthly fees in the $25 range for creating and running a debt management plan. The maximum fees the credit counselor can charge are set by each state.

8. **How are you and your employees paid?** Be wary of agencies that receive commissions for putting people into DMPs.

The Debt Management Plan

Besides budgeting help and advice, the main tool in the credit counseling toolbox is a debt management plan (DMP). Here's how it works.

The agency will contact all of your creditors and gain concessions, usually in the form of lower interest rates for the life of your debt. Creditors will typically also agree to waive late and over-limit fees for the duration of the DMP. This can save you hundreds of dollars over time. Creditors won't reduce your principal in a DMP, so you will end up paying what you owe over the length of the plan.

The agency will look at your income and all of your expenses, down to the level of how much you spend on birthday gifts all year and air-conditioning every summer. It will counsel you to lower your nonessential spending. It will then come up with a monthly amount that you can afford to pay on your debts, and *that* will be the amount it will ask you to pay, in one sum every month to the agency. The agency will parcel it out to your creditors every month until they are paid off.

The typical monthly payment on a DMP is between 2 percent and 3 percent of the outstanding debt. For someone with $26,000 in credit card bills—a typical amount—that means you'd have to come up with between $520 and $780 a month to stay on the plan. But recently a group of major creditors agreed to accept less every month from consumers in particular distress. They said they would accept 1.75 percent a month for hardship clients—those who had lost jobs, or who had major health problems or other reasons why they couldn't qualify for even a traditional DMP. The companies that agreed to that are American Express, Bank of America, Capital One, Chase Card Services, Citibank, Discover Financial Services, GE Money, HSBC Card Services, U.S. Bank, and Wells Fargo Card Services. Someone in the hardship plan with $26,000 of debt would have to pay only $455 a month.

Of course, at that rate of payoff, even with a 6 percent interest rate cap on the charges, it would take more than five years to pay off the debt. The typical length of a debt management plan is 30 months, says Christopher Viale, who adds that at Cambridge Credit most of his clients are done in two years.

If, after adding up all of your debts and analyzing your income and expenses, the credit counseling agency determines that it would take you six years or more to pay off your debts, or if you're not able to even make the minimum payments on a debt management plan, then the DMP may not make sense or help. That's when it's time to talk to a bankruptcy lawyer about your other options.

If you're considering a DMP, you should make sure you keep paying all of your bills while the DMP is being planned and processed. And you should ask these additional questions:

- Is a DMP the only option you can give me? Will you provide me with ongoing budgeting advice, regardless of whether I enroll in a DMP? If an organization offers only DMPs, find another credit counseling organization that also will help you create a budget and teach you money management skills.
- Are there any creditors that won't be covered by this plan? This is an important point that often gets overlooked; you may, even after enrolling in a DMP, have to work out payments to a creditor who is not part of the plan.
- Will I get receipts, or any other notification that all of my creditors are being paid on time? Make sure the counseling

service forwards your money promptly so that all of your bills are paid by the creditor's due dates.

Will a DMP Hurt Your Credit Score?

Being in credit counseling will not hurt your credit score—it may not even show up in your credit report. Being on a debt management plan won't hurt your credit score directly, either, though it is likely to have some impact. That's because typically your existing credit card accounts will be closed as part of the plan. That shows up in your credit file as accounts closed by the creditors, and it lowers your score—a little! As long as you make timely payments under the DMP, your score will continue to reflect that you are an on-time payer. The further in the past that the closed cards recede, the less of an impact there will be on your score. If you are over your head in debt, you should not avoid a DMP because you're afraid of its impact on your score. It's more important that you get the debt dealt with. By the time you are in a position to borrow money again, your scores won't keep you from doing so.

Those Pesky (or Worse) Collection Agents

Somewhere along the way of your debt journey, you're likely to encounter the disturbing phone calls of a collection agent. That means that your creditor has turned your bill over to a third-party agency. In return, the agency will get to keep some percentage— sometimes as high as 60 percent—of the money it wrings out of you. Some agencies just buy debts outright: They pay a small amount for a list of old debts and then get to keep all of the money they actually collect. Collection agents will use a host of techniques—from bothersome phone calls to filing legal suits—to get that money out of you.

You can get hounded by a collection agent even by a debt that is old and no longer collectible—this is called zombie debt. And in recent years, debt collectors have become even more aggressive about hounding people. They use computer algorithms to find out who the most vulnerable names on their lists are; they are filing suit aggressively against borrowers who can't afford lawyers. Because of the paradox that they have a harder time collecting when debt problems are widespread, as they are now, they have become more and more aggressive.

But you can fight back and keep debt collectors in their place, thanks to a slew of regulations governing their behavior. Here's how.

You can dispute a debt. If you're not certain the debt is valid, you can ask the collection agent to verify the debt. It will have to send you a "validation notice" that the credit is legitimate. You then have 30 days to dispute the charge. If there was a dispute about the charge in the first place, the agency will return the debt to the creditor. Robin Leonard, the Nolo Press attorney who specializes in helping people in financial trouble, suggests that if this happens you should follow up to make sure the creditor removes the "sent to collection agency" notation on your credit reports.

You can make them stop calling you. You can ask collection agents to stop contacting you, and they are legally required to do that. Do this with a letter, and in the letter use the words "cease all contact," says Leonard. The agents can still turn around and sue you, if they think it is worth their while to do so. But they can't keep calling and threatening to sue you, or calling you at all.

One consumer lawyer, Robert Stempler, has posted a series of sample letters on his web site for consumers who want to do battle with their creditors and bill collectors. It's worth checking out at www.stopcollectionharassment.com.

Saving Your Home by Fixing Your Loan

In recent years, the housing and mortgage recession had spread so far and wide that mortgage troubles seemed more the norm than the exception. Roughly one in 12 mortgages were delinquent, according to the Mortgage Bankers Association. Every 13 seconds, a new foreclosure was starting, according to the Center for Responsible Lending.

In response to the housing and mortgage pressures that were building, Congress and the Obama administration approved two new mortgage-relief programs designed to help troubled homeowners. These programs are scheduled to expire on June 10, 2010, so it's important, if you're in trouble, to make sure you apply for help before that date. (Though I have to say it would not surprise me if the programs are extended.)

All of the new government programs are organized under the "Making Home Affordable" title. If you're having mortgage troubles, you should start at the web page for that program. It summarizes all of the programs, and offers links to calculators to see if you qualify, as well as links to qualified counselors who can help you navigate these programs. Find all of that at www.makinghomeafford able.gov.

Here are the new government options for troubled homeowners:

Refinancing Plan

If you are stuck in a troubled mortgage, are current on your payments, and want to refinance but can't because you owe more than your house is worth, this plan may be for you. It provides funds for lenders who are willing to refinance your mortgage, even if you owe as much as 125 percent of your home's value. You can use it to get a safe, solid 30-year fixed-rate loan with minimal closing costs. You can't use it to reduce the amount that you owe.

Right now, only loans that are actually held by Fannie Mae or Freddie Mac can qualify for this program, but that's about half of all mortgages out there. You can find out who holds your loan by looking it up here:

- Fannie Mae
  1-800-7FANNIE
  www.fanniemae.com/loanlookup
- Freddie Mac
  1-800-FREDDIE
  www.freddiemac.com/mymortgage

Mortgage Modification Plan

Almost all lenders are now participating in this program, which is aimed at borrowers who are facing unaffordable mortgage payments. If your monthly mortgage costs are more than 31 percent of your monthly gross income and you can't afford to keep making payments, you could qualify.

Under this program, lenders are compensated by the Treasury for allowing you to revise your loan. They will lower your interest rate to the point where your monthly mortgage and related payments total less than 31 percent of your monthly gross income. After a three-month trial period, this rate will be extended for five years. Then your loan will be revisited, and the rate may be raised once more, though it will still be kept at an affordable level. It will be capped there for the remainder of the loan.

You can find out whether your lender is participating in the program by looking up your loan at the Making Home Affordable web site.

Short Sale Plan

Sometimes, you just can't afford to hold on to the home, and you can't sell it, either. You're behind on payments, and your home is worth much less than you still owe. The lender is threatening to foreclose. In this situation, you may be able to do a short sale. This means that you sell the home at the prevailing market value, even though that is less than the amount of the loan, and the lender agrees in advance to take the cash that comes out of that sale as full payment for the loan. When you do a short sale instead of a foreclosure, you can get back into a house of your own far more quickly. Federal lending guidelines stipulate that you need wait only two years to qualify for another mortgage if you do a short sale, but you must wait five to seven years if you go through with a foreclosure.

The Treasury Department is encouraging short sales by paying the lenders $1,000 to accept them, and paying the selling home-owners $1,500 to help with relocation expenses.

Typically, the amount of balance on your mortgage that is for-given by the bank in a short sale is taxable to you. But at the end of 2007, the Bush administration and Congress passed the Mortgage Debt Relief Act of 2007, which exempts that income from taxation. That legislation is good through 2012; after that, forgiven home debt will again be taxable unless the program is extended.

Get the Right Kind of Help

These programs are complex, and it may be hard for homeowners to sort out all of the details and complexities well enough to decide whether they qualify for each program and which one, if any, would be useful for them. But here's another problem: Some of those very same predatory and aggressive mortgage lenders that pushed bad loans on unsuspecting customers, getting them in trouble in the first place, have now hung out "Mortgage Modification Specialist" and "Foreclosure Rescue Specialist" shingles. They are pitching their services as experts in the government programs, and charging people too much money for advice that may be unnecessary or questionable.

One reputable company that has helped thousands of Americans get mortgage modifications or arrange short sales is Home Retention Programs, which you can contact at www.modifymymortgage.com or by calling 800-663-4396. They are run by Jim Richman, who was formerly a commissioner of the national Department of Housing and Urban Development. They will refer you to an attorney in your state who specializes in mortgage modification or short sales. They offer the Pre-Approved Short Sale program, in which your attorney convinces the lender to agree to a specific sale price before your Realtor markets your house, accepts the proceeds of the sale as payment for the house, and eliminates your loan payments during the four to six months that the pending sale is getting approved.

If you want to get help navigating this system, go to one of the government or nonprofit web sites listed next. If you need personal counseling on the issue, use a housing counselor on the Department of Housing and Urban Development's approved list.

You can also go to your servicer (the company to which you currently send your monthly mortgage payment). But in the early months of the mortgage modification plans, most servicers were understaffed and disorganized, so they haven't always been as responsive as they should have been. They are improving.

- **Making Home Affordable:** The main web site housing the Obama administration's mortgage relief programs (www. makinghomeaffordable.gov).
- **Homeownership Preservation Foundation:** A nonprofit that partners with government organizations to help troubled homeowners (www.995hope.org).
- **Homeowner Crisis Resource Center:** Sponsored by the National Foundation for Credit Counseling (www.housinghelp now.org).
- **Foreclosure Avoidance:** The Department of Housing and Urban Development's site listing HUD-approved housing counseling agencies (www.hud.gov/offices/hsg/sfh/hcc/ hcs.cfm).

Foreclosure: The Last Resort

If all else fails—if you are falling behind on payments, have no home equity, can't effect a short sale and can't afford any of the government programs, you may be facing foreclosure. There are strategies for that, too! Strategies that could preserve your house, or at least your ability to afford your next home. A good place to start is with *The Foreclosure Survival Guide*, by Stephen Elias (Nolo, 2008). Stephen outlines the strategies that can help homeowners facing foreclosure.

Once you believe foreclosure is inevitable, stop making your mortgage payments, or even partial payments. Instead, put that money in a savings account that you can use to pay rent on your next home.

The next chapter reveals how you may be able to protect your home by filing for bankruptcy.

You may also be able to negotiate a deal with your lender in which you voluntarily hand over the house before a formal foreclosure document is filed. That may protect your credit score a bit. If you do that, make sure your lender puts in writing that it is willing to accept the home as payment in full for the mortgage loan (short sale).

Staying Healthy without Making Your Bank Account Sick

The most trying financial problems often result from medical bills. Somebody gets sick and has to stop working. Or a family gets desperate to help an ailing family member and uses medical services and treatments that aren't covered by their health insurance. Or they can't find health insurance they can afford.

There are ways to manage your health, and your health care bills, while you wait for Washington to reform the whole health insurance mess.

You can start with obtaining health care coverage. If you were laid off after September 1, 2008, you can continue on your employer's plan for at least nine months at 35 percent of the full cost. The federal government will pick up the rest of the tab, as part of the stimulus bill passed in 2009. Simply ask your employer for that coverage, called COBRA coverage (for Consolidated Omnibus Budget Reconciliation Act, the law that first allowed for the continuation of employer benefits). After the subsidized nine months are up, you can continue taking COBRA benefits for another nine months, but they could get very expensive.

While you're covered under COBRA, you can start looking around for other alternatives and better coverage. You can look for a private health insurance policy online at www.ehealthinsurance. com, an online brokerage that represents most health insurers. The National Association of Insurance Commissioners suggests that you check its web site (www.naic.org) to see if your state has its own risk pool for people who can't qualify for other insurance or just need temporary insurance.

Medical Repricing

I have my own solution to the health insurance dilemma, which I developed with the help of Assurant health insurance and the Consumers Direct Association of America. You can find it at www.medicalrepricing.com, or call (877) 642-5657. My idea was that you could save money on your health insurance and health care costs if you could do three things:

1. Use a high-deductible health insurance plan that covers catastrophes but keeps monthly premiums low. Catastrophic major medical coverage will protect you from the crushing financial burdens of medical conditions that require hospitalization or other forms of expensive medical treatment. A high-deductible policy doesn't cover every scratch or sniffle the way a low-deductible plan does, but it costs much less in premiums.
2. Negotiate lower fees with medical providers. My plan includes a medical repricing card, which gets you discounts from providers, and typically costs less than $35 a month for the whole family.
3. Get good prices on basic preventive care so you are covered for regular checkups, mammograms, and the like. This third component is a scheduled benefits plan. It provides significant coverage for the common everyday expenses like doctor visits, prescriptions, and other expenses not covered by the high deductible on your catastrophic major medical policy.

You can buy any one of those three pieces by itself, and there may be times when that is appropriate for you. But when you put all three together, they work to cut your costs, cover your catastrophes, *and* save you money. You can get all of the details at www.medicalrepricing.com.

(Continued)

What about Those Medical Bills?

Maybe you already have had a medical emergency or problem and are drowning in hospital and doctor bills. You can often negotiate these bills after the fact—hospitals do have money set aside for hardship cases. But talking the hospital into putting you on their hardship list can be challenging—almost as challenging as getting your health insurer to pay up when it is supposed to.

So I am going to recommend that you call in help. If you have medical bills you can't pay, or have a stack of bills you lack the emotional strength to work your way through, hire a health care advocate who will negotiate all of this for you.

I'm a fan of Kevin Flynn and his HealthCare Advocates organization. When Kevin was 18, he was hit by a car and severely injured. He had brain injuries that caused him to lose his memory—including his memory of how to do things like walk, talk, read, write, and do math. He spent three years fighting back and has triumphed over his medical challenges. But along the way, he found himself frustrated by the high cost of his treatment, and he discovered some secret low-cost ways of getting care.

So he started HealthCare Advocates (www.healthcareadvocates.com, or call 215-735-7711) in Philadelphia, where he lives. His company will do these things to make sure his clients don't pay any more than they have to for health care:

- **Medical referrals.** HealthCare Advocates offers referrals to doctors and hospitals that are experts in their field and that charge reasonable rates.
- **Insurance negotiations.** Kevin Flynn and his team will negotiate exclusions, such as preexisting conditions, out of their clients' health insurance agreements.
- **Medical bill negotiations.** The firm will go back to providers you've already seen and win reductions in billed amounts.

Flynn and his team have talked insurance companies into paying for hospital stays, speech therapies, and surgeries they originally denied, and he has gotten hospitals to cancel or reduce their bills. He charges on a sliding scale, based on how many different providers are billing you and how complex your situation is, but the typical charge for the typical client fighting bills from three different providers is $400.

Of course, HealthCare Advocates isn't the only company like this around, though it has been nationally recognized. Another big player in this field is the Patient Advocate Foundation in Newport News, Virginia (www.patientadvocate.org).

If you're looking for an advocate to help you with your medical finances, just make sure you find one with good consumer recommendations, a complaint-free record with your state's consumer affairs office, and a long history of being in the business. This is a field that can be very volatile; some people get into it, find it too hard, and leave. And having your medical advocate go out of business with your money adds insult to injury, literally.

CHAPTER
11

Surviving Bankruptcy

Longtime *Newsweek* financial columnist Jane Bryant Quinn recently departed from her long-held views about debt and made the case for walking away. "I'll risk my good-girl reputation with a subversive idea: go bankrupt," she said. "If you're reaching the end of your rope, don't try to hold on. Save what you can."

Jane's column was a shocking commentary on the state of the American consumer. Lenders pushed bad loans on anyone willing to sign, credit card issuers piled fees and interest on top of intransigent balances, and people met every challenge, from $4 gas to a medical emergency, with more borrowing. Just as everyone was getting really overextended, the bottom fell out of the housing market, too many jobs evaporated in the recession, and new credit dried up. It was as if the system was stacked against people who wanted to do the right thing and pay off their debts.

I agree with her. If you can't afford a debt management plan, if you're behind on your mortgage and you can't see your way out, bankruptcy is a reasonable option. It will offer you relief from the calls, the bills, and the middle-of-the-night worries about debt. It will ruin your ability to borrow money, but only for 7 to 10 years and possibly less. It will enable you to protect some of your assets, such as your retirement account and possibly your house.

And it will put you in good company. Many famous and ultimately successful people have filed for bankruptcy protection—including actress Kim Basinger, tennis star Bjorn Borg, movie producer/director Francis Ford Coppola, Walt Disney, country singer Merle Haggard, and billionaire entrepreneur Donald Trump.

Moreover, hardworking, ethical, and smart middle-class people are pushed into bankruptcy every day. At least half the time, health problems and medical bills are what put them over the top. Recently, well over one million people have filed for bankruptcy every year, according to the American Bankruptcy Institute.

So, don't waste time feeling alone or feeling bad. Do what you have to do to protect yourself and your family from drowning. You can emerge from bankruptcy with a financial life and with honor—and your retirement accounts. (You can even voluntarily pay those creditors you really want to pay, after your bankruptcy is discharged.) You may even be able to emerge with your house, as I'll explain later in this chapter. Just make sure you do it right. Paying too much for bankruptcy, filing the wrong way, or bringing an unethical adviser in to supposedly help you with your bankruptcy can just compound the pain.

In this chapter, I lay out what you need to know to file for bankruptcy and emerge better and stronger than ever.

There Are Two Forms of Consumer Bankruptcy

Consumers filing for personal nonbusiness bankruptcy protection have two basic choices for the kind of bankruptcy they file, named for their sections of the United States bankruptcy code.

1. **Chapter 7** bankruptcy is a liquidation bankruptcy. In a Chapter 7 bankruptcy, the court will sell many of your assets and wipe out all of your debts, but you still can often keep your home, your car, and a large sum of money in your retirement accounts. A Chapter 7 bankruptcy takes three months and stays in your credit file for 10 years, and you are prohibited from filing another Chapter 7 bankruptcy for eight years.
2. **Chapter 13** bankruptcy is often called a "wage earner's bankruptcy." It is a reorganization bankruptcy, in which the court will approve your plan for using your expected salary to pay off some portion of your existing debts over three to five years. Some debts, such as child support, must be paid in full, while others, such as credit card debts, can often be paid off at pennies on the dollar in a Chapter 13 bankruptcy. A Chapter 13 bankruptcy stays in your credit file for seven years, and you

can file a Chapter 7 bankruptcy six years after filing a Chapter 13 bankruptcy.

Which Is Better—Chapter 7 or Chapter 13?

- **Choose Chapter 7** if your situation is so severe that you want to walk away from all of your debts, and if your income is low for your state (see the means test discussion on page 172). If you haven't missed a mortgage payment and want to try to keep your house, choose Chapter 7.
- **Choose Chapter 13** if you are a high earner and want more time to pay off your debts. If you have fallen behind on your mortgage and want to keep your house, choose Chapter 13.

Why doesn't everyone choose Chapter 7? If you're behind on your mortgage payments but think you can catch up and want to keep your house, you can do that with a Chapter 13 filing and not a Chapter 7 filing.

But the main reason why many consumers don't go Chapter 7 is because they aren't allowed to. Congress passed the Bankruptcy Abuse Prevention and Consumer Protection Act of 2005—a law that closed the Chapter 7 door for many middle-class people. It added a means test, so that only low earners can use the liquidation bankruptcy. If you make too much and try to file Chapter 7, you can get forced into Chapter 13.

That law has certainly had an impact. In 2005, the final year before the law went into effect, some 1.6 million consumers filed for Chapter 7 bankruptcy protection, about four times the number of people who went Chapter 13. The following year, there were 349,012 Chapter 7 filings and 238,430 Chapter 13 filings. Filings were down overall because (1) many people on the brink had accelerated their filings the year before, (2) the economy was relatively strong, and (3) lawyers started charging more money to prepare bankruptcy filings after the law went into effect.

With the economic troubles of recent years, more consumers are again able to qualify for Chapter 7. In 2008, Chapter 7 filings topped 714,380, about twice the number of Chapter 13 filings.

The Chapter 7 Means Test

The income test for filing Chapter 7 bankruptcy is complicated, and "very unfair," according to Stephen Elias, one of the nation's foremost bankruptcy experts and author of *The New Bankruptcy: Will It Work for You?* (Nolo, 2009). Stephen contends that the formula used to qualify people for Chapter 7 bankruptcy is skewed in such a way that it helps rural families and hurts city dwellers (who often have higher incomes for their state).

The first step is seeing whether your current monthly income exceeds the median income for a household of your size in your state. If your income is under that level, you can typically file Chapter 7. If it is over that level, a second means test applies. It mainly exists to see whether you're in a position to afford to pay off debts under a Chapter 13 plan, and it is locale-specific. Stephen has set up a web site that allows you to see whether you'd pass the means test at www. legalconsumer.com/bankruptcy/nolo/.

If you are self-employed and report your business income as sole-proprietor income on your income tax forms, that income will also be subject to the same means test. Don't think you can quit your job just to qualify yourself for a Chapter 7 filing—the court can view that as fraud and refuse to accept your filing.

Get Help

Bankruptcy is a highly technical legal proceeding, and you don't want to go through it without some expert advice, even if you eventually decide to file the papers by yourself.

- **Get credit counseling.** The 2005 law requires that you undergo credit counseling before you file for bankruptcy—you can't file unless you present a certificate showing you've completed credit counseling from an approved agency. To find a list of credit counseling agencies approved by the Justice Department to fulfill this obligation, go to this web site: www.usdoj. gov/ust/eo/bapcpa/ccde/cc_approved.htm.
- **Get legal help.** There is a national network of free and inexpensive bankruptcy law clinics staffed by attorneys who can help you review your situation and file the right papers in the right way. The American Bankruptcy Institute offers an interactive map on its web site that lists all of the attorneys and

legal clinics offering free advice and filing assistance to consumers. Find it at http://probono.abiworld.org/.

Before You File

Once you believe you are heading for a bankruptcy filing, there are certain moves you should make to protect your assets, and safeguard your finances going forward. Do talk to a lawyer, and do learn about how various assets and debts are disposed of during bankruptcy. Don't try to hide assets or give valuable items to your relatives for safekeeping: Bankruptcy can be depressing enough without adding fraud to your filing.

There are legal steps you can take to make your postbankruptcy life easier. For example:

- You should continue to make payments on your mortgage to keep that loan current, if you are able to and want to emerge from bankruptcy with your house.
- You may want to stop making payments on nonsecured loans, including credit cards. The bankruptcy trustee charged with liquidating your assets can call back any payments you make that are over $600 in the three months before your filing.
- Feed your IRA. Most bankruptcy proceedings protect your retirement savings up to $1 million. Instead of using what spare cash you might have to try to keep up with bills, deposit it in your IRA.
- Be careful about using your credit cards. You can't load up on consumer goods just before you file, thinking it's your last chance to buy jewelry or take a vacation. Credit card charges of $500 or more for luxury goods or services made within 90 days prior to bankruptcy or cash advances totaling $750 or more taken within 70 days are considered nondischargeable debts.
- You can sell valuable things that you own, such as jewelry or electronics, and use the proceeds to pay down secured loans, such as your car loan or your home loan. This will prevent those items from being sold later to pay off your nonsecured loans.
- Don't move. You have to have lived in a state for 90 days before you are eligible to file for bankruptcy in that state. If you want to protect more than $125,000 of equity in your house, you

have to have lived in it (or another home in the same state) for
40 months before your bankruptcy filing.

What about Your House?

Both forms of consumer bankruptcy provide ways that allow you to
keep your house in some circumstances, but it isn't always feasible.

If you have a lot of equity in your home, you may be forced to sell
it to satisfy your debts under a Chapter 7 filing—or you may not.
Every state has different rules about how much house it will allow you
to keep; this is called a homestead exemption. In some places that is
determined by a dollar figure; in others it has to do with the size
of the property. Having a spouse on the home's title will also affect
how much of the home's equity can be protected. It's good to get
legal advice in your own state about this, but you can find a list of all
of the homestead exemptions on Stephen Elias's web site, at www
.legalconsumer.com.

A Chapter 13 bankruptcy can protect your home if you're able to
pay the mortgage. You can amortize any missed payments into your
repayment plan to catch up with the payments.

If you are behind on your mortgage and the home is worth less
than you owe on it, you are "upside down" or "underwater" in
creditors' jargon. In that situation, you may not want to keep your
home. But it will be on a separate track from the rest of your assets
and liabilities—the company owning the mortgage may put you into
foreclosure, a separate procedure from bankruptcy (and one dealt
with in Chapter 10).

What Happens When You File

Once you make your initial bankruptcy filing, all of your creditors
need to back off; you get an automatic stay that prevents them from
continuing to try to collect money from you.

During that period, even your mortgage company and car loan
company will have to let you be: They can't foreclose or repossess
while your bankruptcy is in process.

A Chapter 7 filing will require you to inventory all of your assets
and your liabilities and make a brief appearance in court. The court
will appoint a trustee, who will sell your assets, pay what is possible on

your debts, and discharge them. Every state also has a list of exemptions that the trustee will let you keep—typically personal items and household goods that are more useful than they are valuable. That process typically takes three months and you emerge with a fresh start, mostly. Some debts, including taxes, student loans, and child support, will not be discharged.

If you file a Chapter 13 bankruptcy, you and your lawyer will have to come up with a repayment plan that satisfies the judge. For the most part, you can keep your assets under a Chapter 13 filing. Once the judge approves your plan to reduce your debts and stretch out your payments, it will become official and you'll be supervised by the bankruptcy court for the three to five years it takes for you to complete your debt-paydown plan.

Before your debts are discharged, you will have to take a debtor education course from a Justice Department–approved provider. Find them here: www.usdoj.gov/ust/eo/bapcpa/ccde/de_approved.htm.

Life after Bankruptcy

"Once you are out of bankruptcy, your credit histories will be ruined and your FICO (Fair Isaac Corporation) scores will be low, low, low," writes John Ventura in his excellent book, *The Bankruptcy Handbook* (Kaplan Publishing, 2008). Nevertheless, life goes on, and yours will, too.

For a while, at least, you'll have to lead a cash-based life. You may even want to sell some assets you were able to protect during bankruptcy to get money to live on and to build up an emergency fund.

Do what it takes to stay on the straight and narrow and live below your means: If you feel like you need more help with budgeting, you can continue to get counseling from a nonprofit agency, or you can join a self-help group such as Debtors Anonymous (www.debtorsanonymous.org or call 800-421-2383).

You may feel like you want to pay some debts that were discharged during your bankruptcy filing. For example, you may want to pay your doctor or your favorite local merchant money you owed them before you went bankrupt. There is no legal requirement that you do this. It's strictly voluntary, and it does have a downside: Reactivating a debt that was discharged in bankruptcy starts that debt's clock rolling again. It can appear as new on your credit report, and if you again fall behind, it can damage your report and your score well into the future. If it makes you feel better to repay those debts and you can afford to do so, go ahead and do it, but do it carefully. Send money voluntarily to your creditor, but don't sign a new promissory note or agree to any formal payment plan.

Rebuilding Your Credit Score

Your ability to borrow money may come back to you sooner than your ability to handle it, so make sure you are spending less than you are earning and managing it well, before you start borrowing any more money.

But you may find yourself approved for secured debt, such as car loans, as quickly as two years after your bankruptcy filing.

You'll not get a new credit card as quickly, but you can start to rebuild your credit file with a secured credit card, as I explained in Chapter 7.

With every year that your bankruptcy filing recedes into the past, your new accounts and payments will build your credit score back up. After seven (or 10) years have lapsed, your bankruptcy will disappear entirely.

In the meantime, hold your head up. Bankruptcy is legal and legitimate for a reason—it's a structured way for people who have been buried (in no small part by abusive lending practices) to emerge whole, safe, and sound. You can use the fresh start that bankruptcy gives you to build a new life—one in which you don't lose sleep at night worrying about money, and in which you can contribute to your family and society in the ways you most want to. After all, Mark Twain did his best work after his bankruptcy filing.

12

Debt Strategies for Every Age

If you've been reading this book sequentially, you'll have picked up a number of smart strategies for mastering your debt by now. I've shared my best credit card and mortgage tips, ideas for paying down debt fast and saving money on health care, car, and student loans.

But not every strategy makes sense for every stage of life. A refinance that adds 30 years to the length of your mortgage may not make sense for a near-retiree. Using a credit card to buy a car can be financial suicide for a new graduate.

You'll do best if you focus on the financial tasks that are most important for each stage of life. Here's an age-and-stage guide to mastering debt, wherever you are. You'll find the specifics for each checklist item elsewhere in this book.

In Your Teens and 20s: Clean Living

The single most important move you can make as you are beginning your financial life is this: Learn about money. Reading this book is a great start. Check out the resources at the back of the book, and do more studying on your own. Think of it this way: You probably have spent more than a dozen years taking math, or Spanish, or history. That has prepared you for some tasks and for more study. Learn about borrowing, budgeting, spending, and investing, and it will come back to you in the form of dollars saved and earned over your entire life. Here are other money strategies for 20-somethings.

- **Use money.** Get a checking account and debit card as soon as you have a job (even if it's a babysitting gig) and start earning money. Get your parents to help you open the account, if necessary. Learn to deposit and save, withdraw and spend.

- **Build credit.** Once you've got that down, get a credit card. Following recent credit card legislation, you may need to get your parents to cosign the card with you. That is okay, but you should manage the card, get the bills, and pay them, even if you are doing so from an allowance while you are in college. Use the card as a convenience instead of carrying cash, and pay it off in full every month. Keep your credit limit low until you're comfortable working with your card.

- **Limit student loans.** Think three times or more before you sign up for any costly private loans, especially if you're not sure what you want to do after college. Comparison shop for the student loans you do take out. Remember that paying them back could crimp your postcollege choices.

- **Start saving for short-term goals.** You will need a decent credit score and an extra couple of months' rent to get your first apartment, and you will need money to furnish it. It's hard to save while you are also building your first professional wardrobe and commuting to your first low-paying job. But the more cash you accumulate, the better—especially of you want to position yourself to buy your first home. In this tough new mortgage era, you will definitely need a down payment.

- **Add other debts.** As you move through your 20s, you'll probably sign for your first car loan, and possibly for your first home loan. All of that will help you to build a solid credit file. And *that* will help you to borrow more money less expensively in the future.

- **Get health insurance.** Even if you have to pay for it yourself, you should have health insurance. Even invincible athletes can sustain injuries. You aren't just protecting the few bucks in your bank account; you're buying access to better health care. And you're protecting your parents' future, too: If you *did* have a health emergency and no health insurance, you know they'd probably step in and help, even if they couldn't really afford it. Until recently, insurance companies typically removed kids from their parents' insurance plans as soon as they graduated from college or turned 24. But many states have passed laws allowing parents to keep their children on their health insurance plans until they are as old as 30. Check the rules in your state.

- **Start to invest.** Use a Roth individual retirement account if your taxable income is not very high. Put at least enough into your employer 401(k), 403(b), or 457 plan to make sure you get the full benefit of company matching contributions.

- **Be rigorous about paying bills on time and not borrowing too much.** I hear from so many young people who get in serious, serious trouble before they even understand what they've done. Then it takes years to climb out. Protect your future.

The 30s and 40s: Building Wealth, Getting Squeezed

These middle years may be ones in which your career finally feels like it is clicking, but you probably still feel squeezed. No wonder: You have to figure out how to pay for everything from soccer shoes to sofas to retirement contributions. Your parents may be looking to you for help. The central financial task for this time of your life? Setting sensible priorities and sticking with them. When you decide what you really want to say yes to, it's easier to know what to say no to. Other debt management moves for the middle years:

- **Stay on top of your credit cards and other consumer debts.** Terms change annually, so at least once a year review all of your accounts and make sure you are getting the best deals. Don't be afraid to shuffle balances from one account to another if it gets you closer to your financial goals.
- **Expect a lot from your mortgage.** If you don't love the loan you have, consider refinancing. Determine whether you want to put yourself on a schedule for paying it off early.
- **Apply for a home equity line of credit.** Even if you don't use it right away, it's useful to have this borrowing power at your fingertips. And when you need it, you may not be able to qualify.
- **Borrow and spend money for appreciating assets, not depreciating ones.** Skimp on your car, if you must, to make your mortgage payment and your retirement contribution.
- **Invest, invest, invest.** Invest in retirement accounts and in your own career via continuing education, business equipment, and other expenses that will make you money in the future.
- **Help set your kids up for college.** Establish Coverdell or 529 college savings plans for them. When grandparents and other relatives ask for gift advice, point them in that direction.
- **Protect your family.** That usually means having adequate general policies for life, health, home, auto, and disability

insurance. It usually *doesn't* mean having specialized policies aimed at everything from cancer to credit cards.

In Your 50s: Countdown to Retirement

It's a good idea to become debt free before you retire, and that's true even if you can afford payments on a good mortgage. Here's why: If you expect to be supporting yourself in retirement on withdrawals from a tax-deferred account, such as a 401(k) plan or individual retirement account, you'll pay income taxes on every amount you withdraw. Furthermore, those withdrawals are likely to raise your total income over $34,000 ($44,000 for couples)—the point at which 80 percent of your Social Security benefits are taxable as income. So, if you are withdrawing money monthly to pay your mortgage, you're spending extra every month.

As you move toward your empty-nest and retirement years, your central financial task is setting your financial life up so that it will afford you the retirement you want.

- Get serious about paying off your mortgage and other loans.
- Invest in a variety of savings vehicles, including taxable accounts as well as tax-deferred retirement accounts.
- Help your children through college, but don't take on debt you can't afford in order to do that. They will have other options, including less expensive schools and long lifetimes to pay off their own loans. If you are moving toward retirement, you may not have the time to pay off costly college obligations.
- Use a home equity line of credit or refinanced mortgage to do the home repairs you think you will need before you retire. Once you retire, you may not be able to borrow, or pay back, this money.
- Consider buying your retirement home early. Mortgage rates and home prices look attractive now, especially in retirement areas that were very hard hit. You could buy that place in Florida and have it close to paid off before you move there— but *only* if you're really sure you want to move to Florida.

The 60s and Beyond: Early Retirement

Once you have stopped working, you are in a different financial world. You may not be able to borrow money easily, even if you have solid savings and retirement account balances. If you still have debts, you may have a harder time paying them back.

You may also find yourself losing employer-provided health insurance before Medicare kicks in. Your financial tasks at this age? Using your money to enjoy the early years of retirement without sapping your savings.

- **Decide when to start taking Social Security benefits.** It's often a good idea to delay starting your benefits as long as possible, because you'll get a higher monthly benefit as long as you live. Some couples find its best for one spouse—the low earner—to start benefits as soon as possible, at age 62, and have the other spouse delay benefits as long as possible. Of course, this is a lifestyle decision and not just a financial one. The Social Security Administration's web site offers calculators that can help you see the effects of starting or delaying benefits, at www.ssa.gov/planners.

- **Carefully analyze any loans you have outstanding.** If you have money in the bank and an outstanding mortgage, you may prefer to keep it that way, especially if you can make the mortgage payments on your retirement income and your mortgage rate is low. But you may be better off simply paying off your balances and not worrying about them. You can decide that on a financial basis, by looking at the interest rates on your outstanding loans and on the income you are earning from your savings. If you're paying high interest but earning little, paying off your loans may make sense. If, however, you're happy with your investments and your mortgage interest rates are low and fixed, keeping the loan could be the better choice.

- **Make the most of credit card rewards programs.** If you're comfortably affording your lifestyle and that lifestyle includes frequent travel, take advantage of rewards programs. Find the mileage or cash-back card that suits you best and use it to the max. Pay it off every month and watch your free trips accumulate.

- **Bankruptcy may offer you more options than it does to younger borrowers.** Of course, by now it would be better to not be buried in debt. But retirees have an easier time going through bankruptcy: Up to $1 million of their IRA balances are off-limits to creditors. If you are bumping up against the Social

Security years and really are deeply in debt, talk to a bankruptcy attorney. It may provide the relief you need for the next stage of life.

- **Keep your health insurance.** If you lose your employer's plan, buy it privately. You can sign up for Medicare three months before your 65th birthday; at that time you should start shopping for a Medigap policy as well.
- **Consider lending money to needy relatives.** If your parents or your children are asking you for cash, consider formalizing a loan arrangement. Done right—with relatives who *will* pay you back—you can increase your income while decreasing the amount of interest they will pay.

Over 75: The Second Half of Retirement

You'll have to make lifestyle decisions again once you've hit the slower, later years of retirement. Of course you will still enjoy activities and hobbies, but you may find that the house is too much for you. Or you may find you want to stay put.

- **Live on your house.** Most homeowners do eventually tap the equity in their home to pay for their later years of life. There are three main ways to do that: (1) sell your home and invest the money you receive, (2) take out a reverse mortgage that will let you take cash out of the house while you stay in it, or (3) take out a home equity loan if you still qualify. Some families work out other alternatives: Either the kids move in with their mom and help cover her expenses in exchange for free rent, or the mom sells her home and uses some of the proceeds to have living space built for herself at her children's home. All of these possibilities have pros and cons; what's important is studying the ramifications and choosing the best one for you.
- **Protect your nest egg.** Older people are the top targets for scams of every sort. Their identities may get stolen, or they may be sold fake products, or they may be asked to contribute to questionable charities. Follow the same smart strategy you've used all of your life: Ask questions, do the research, and avoid any financial deal that doesn't make sense to you.

CHAPTER

13

Permanent Mastery, Going Forward

There are many facts, figures, statements, and strategies in this book, but none is truer than this: The financial marketplace is always changing, and it always will continue to change. The choices, products, interest rates, and situations you are facing now are different than they were when I began work on this book. They may even be different than they were when you started reading Chapter 1.

Those changes can come from any direction. They can come from Washington, where new policies, laws, and regulations change the way lenders and borrowers do business. They can come from Wall Street, where big institutional investors can determine which products banks keep, and which ones they abandon. The changes can come from your own neighborhood, where local rules, regulations, and consumer demand can create or kill the market for particular products. And they can come from your own house, where a job change, a wedding, a leaky roof, or a new family room can change your financial needs.

The most important lesson then, is this: Stay informed. Be nimble. Don't assume that what worked last year will work now. Review your situation—and the financial marketplace—regularly. Consider yourself a lifetime user of credit tools, always on the watch for the next money-saving product and strategy.

What I'd most like to leave you with, then, is not a hard-and-fast set of rules to live by, but a set of skills and some core principles. Along with the right attitude, these will ensure that you can thrive in whatever marketplace exists as you move forward.

Attitude Is All

If you approach your financial future with the right attitude, you'll succeed and thrive. Remember that the financial marketplace needs you at least as much as you need it. Those brokers, bankers, and loan peddlers are pitching to you in the hopes that you will buy their products. They compete with each other and with other products and services for your dollar. *You* are in charge.

Own that power and embrace it. If someone tries to sell you on a product you don't understand, make them explain it until you do, or go elsewhere. If a bank you've long dealt with persists in piling on fees and hidden expenses you think are unfair, find another bank. If a poor credit score is keeping you from refinancing your mortgage, make the moves that will force the credit scoring companies to raise your score. You are the boss.

Don't allow anyone—even, especially, you—to make you feel bad about your financial circumstances. So many good, smart, and hardworking people have gotten into money troubles that were not of their own making—bad products, predatory lending, and a generally out-of-whack economy all contributed to the troubles that have been so widespread. Even if you made mistakes (and who hasn't, at one time or another?), don't beat yourself up; just fix them and move on.

Think of money and debt as emotionally neutral tools to be used. Tackle credit card offers and new government programs as if they were Sudoku puzzles to be solved. Challenge yourself.

Feel strong and smart, *act* strong and smart, and you will be able to master money in a whole new way. Have faith that you can improve your financial situation, no matter what it is, and move on to prosper—regardless of what the economy throws at you.

Polish Your Skills

You can teach yourself to be good with money and debt, just as you taught yourself to tie your shoes, ride a bike, and pass high school algebra. Here are the skills that will bring you financial mastery.

- **Research.** You don't need to know everything. You just need to know where to find the answers. Happily, today they are all over the Internet, for free. You'll find a list of my favorite financial resources in the Appendix to this book. Spend some time checking them out, and choose your favorites. Remember to notice who sponsors a web site as you study its contents, and you can learn from all of them. Set aside as little as 15 minutes a week to teach yourself something new about credit, debt, and money. You really are never too old to learn the facts of financial life, and the more you'll learn, the more facile you will become.

Learn to do the research necessary to comparison shop financial products. That includes reading, asking questions, and studying the small print.

- **Math.** At its core, credit is a numbers game, and you can, and often should, make those decisions on the basis of numbers. Which card should you pay off first? Which loan is cheaper? These are questions that have numerical answers. Happily, you don't have to do all the math yourself—the Internet is replete with financial calculators. But you should understand how those numbers work together. Understand compounding: Interest piled onto itself grows and grows. Change interest rates into decimals—4 percent equals 0.04—so you can quickly calculate annual interest costs of one offer over another. Play with the numbers, play with the calculators, and you'll make more fully informed decisions going forward.
- **Record keeping.** Find a system that works for you and use it to track your regular expenses and your debts and assets. Without a good handle on this information, you can't make good decisions.
- **Decision making.** Train yourself to make good financial decisions by studying the options and the facts and being decisive. Make decisions based on the numbers and on your long-term personal goals. Remember that not making decisions—sitting in a bad loan or hiding from a debt you can't pay—is the same thing as making a bad decision.
- **Discipline.** All of this isn't easy. Sometimes you have to choose between two contradictory financial goals, or give up things that may seem very important to you and your family, to get your finances on the right path. If you practice and employ the skill of financial discipline, you will reap rewards.
- **Self-soothing.** For lack of a better word, it is good to have the skill of being able to calm yourself when you are worrying about money. There are all kinds of techniques that work for

different people. For some, a yoga session or trip to the gym might help. Others control worry by setting aside a time and place to worry, say for 15 minutes a day, and putting the worries aside at other times. You can write a list of alternative ways you could come up with extra money if you had to—everything from the garage sale to the weekend babysitting gig. It also helps, when you are worrying about money, to think about the people you most admire in life, and to realize that they are rarely the people with the most money.

Guiding Principles

The marketplace changes, but certain financial truths remain eternal. At least in my book—and that's what this is!

Here are the principles I think you should always remember as you continue to revise and improve your finances. Take them to heart, and you will truly be a debt master.

- **There are no dumb questions.** If any financial adviser or salesperson ever tries to convince you that a product is too complex for you to understand, run in the other direction. Ask away until you know what you are getting into. Don't ever pretend you understand something that you don't understand because you don't want to look dumb. Scamsters count on that.
- **The devil is in the details.** Laws and regulations come and go, but companies *always* try to hide the bad parts in the small print. Read all of your terms and agreements carefully.
- **Follow the money.** Whenever financial experts are being compensated to sell you a product, they are not on your side. Trust yourself, consumer groups, and educational organizations for impartial information—not the person who is going to make big money if you take out a particular loan or sign up for a particular service. You can't always avoid paying a commission, but when you understand who is paid and how much, you'll have a better understanding of the deal.
- **Pay off costliest debt first.** It feels great to be debt free. The best way to get there is to make extra payments to your most expensive debts, which are likely to be credit cards. Pay them off in order of how high their interest rates are.

- **Borrow for appreciating assets, not depreciating ones.** If you can afford the payments, it's still worth borrowing money to buy a home, build a business, or get a college education. Those items will eventually earn money for you. The loan enables you to take advantage of the opportunity to earn money. A car, a couch, a big-screen TV? Not so much. You may have to borrow to afford a car, and you may need a car to get to work, so that loan may be necessary. But borrowing money to buy things you can't afford to pay cash for is generally not a good idea.
- **Don't lie to yourself about money.** It really doesn't help for very long. And you can't correct a situation unless you're clear about what that situation is.
- **The bottom line is the one to watch.** The true cost of a debt is complex and not just about the interest rate. Calculate the total cost of the debt over time, including fees, points, interest, and opportunities presented or lost, whenever you are analyzing a loan.

That's it. Hold these principles firm and keep your finances flexible enough to respond to the ever-changing environment. You don't have to do everything all at once; just resolve to do a little at a time. Learn about debt, replace bad products with better ones, keep up with rules changes, and use the resources on the following pages to get help with all of those tasks. You'll be a debt master before you know it.

A P P E N D I X

Resources

There are an abundance of good sources of information on debt management and mastery. Here are some of my favorites:

General Resources

The organizations, web sites, and books in this category are good all-around resources for financial information. They tend to cover everything from credit card rates to reverse mortgages.

- Federal Trade Commission
  600 Pennsylvania Avenue, NW
  Washington, DC 20580
  (202) 326-2222
  www.ftc.gov

  The FTC has reams of information on its web site about identity theft, credit card practices, and more.

- Bankrate
  www.bankrate.com

  A great first click for questions about credit. In addition to current interest rates for all sorts of loans, this site includes many terrific calculators and worksheets.

- Nolo Press
  950 Parker Street
  Berkeley, CA 94710-2524
  (800) 728-3555
  www.nolo.com

Nolo Press is a self-help law publishing firm, staffed by smart and compassionate lawyers. It is excellent. It offers thorough guides through debt relief, bankruptcy, and everything else from writing a will to starting a business. It also offers online help, form letters, and software so you can be your own lawyer.

- Kiplinger Washington Editors
1729 H Street, NW
Washington, DC 20006
(800) 544-0155
www.kiplinger.com

Kiplinger's Personal Finance is perhaps the best real-life personal finance magazine. The Kiplinger.com web site boasts lots of up-to-date advice and many good calculators and worksheets.

- MSN Money
http://moneycentral.msn.com/home.asp

A thorough, comprehensive web site about all matters financial.

- CNN Money
http://money.cnn.com/pf/

Another comprehensive web site; includes content from *Money* magazine.

- Credit.com
www.credit.com

A credit education and monitoring firm staffed by folks who have a lot of expertise and consumer credentials.

Calculators

These two web sites have excellent financial calculators that can help you work out answers for just about any money question you can face.

1. Financial Calculators from KJE Computer Solutions: www.dinkytown.net/
2. Moneychimp: www.moneychimp.com

Books

- *The Difference: How Anyone Can Prosper in Even the Toughest Times*, by Jean Chatzky (Crown Business, 2009). An excellent overview on sound money behavior.
- *Credit Repair*, by Robin Leonard and John Lamb (Nolo, 2009). This classic offers sound advice on how to fix debt problems and manage credit reports. It includes several sample letters within the book and on a CD that is packaged with the book.
- *I Will Teach You to Be Rich*, by Ramit Sethi (Workman Publishing, 2009). Clever, straightforward advice about the breadth of spending and borrowing, from the founder of the blog by the same name at www.iwillteachyoutoberich.com.
- *Get a Financial Life*, by Beth Kobliner (Fireside, 2009). An excellent book, updated with new material, aimed at 20- and 30-somethings.
- *Deal with Your Debt*, by Liz Pulliam Weston (Pearson Education, 2006). The author does a good job of explaining how to proceed when you want to start digging out of financial trouble.
- *Managing Debt for Dummies*, by John Ventura and Mary Reed (Wiley Publishing, 2007). A decent, general overview of how to manage consumer debt.

Topical Resources

These resources address specific topics that are covered in this book.

Money Management and Budgeting

These are all computer-based or online software programs designed to let you track and budget your spending. Try a few, and see which one you like best.

- Quicken, from Intuit: available at www.quicken.com
- Microsoft MoneyPlus: www.microsoft.com/money
- Buxfer: www.buxfer.com
- Green Sherpa: www.greensherpa.com
- Mint: www.mint.com
- Money Strands: www.moneystrands.com
- Wesabe: www.wesabe.com

Credit Cards

- *How You Can Profit from Credit Cards,* by Curtis E. Arnold (FT Press, 2008). Soup to nuts, everything you need to know about credit cards from the publisher of CardRatings, www.credit cardperks.com, an educational web site.
- *Talk Your Way Out of Credit Card Debt,* by Scott Bilker (Press One Publishing, 2003). This oldie but goodie teaches you how to be a tough negotiator when you are dealing with your card issuer.
- Debt Smart: www.debtsmart.com

    The web site of Scott Bilker, who offers techniques for negotiating with your credit card company.

Credit Card Web Sites   All of these sites are good places to compare credit card offers and catch the latest news on card rates:

- CardRatings: www.creditcardperks.com
- Index Credit Cards: www.indexcreditcards.com
- Low Cards: http://lowcards.com
- CardTrak: www.cardtrak.com

Credit Reporting Agencies

- Equifax
  (800) 685-1111
  www.guardmycredit.com
- Experian
  (888) 397-3742
  www.experian.com
- TransUnion
  (800) 888-4213
  www.transunion.com

Credit Monitoring

These are sites where you can follow your credit reports and scores.

- Annual Credit Report: www.annualcreditreport.com. This is the one true free site for getting your credit report from each of the three credit reporting agencies.

- TrueCredit, from TransUnion: www.truecredit.com
- Experian: www.freecreditreport.com
- Equifax: www.equifax.com
- Credit Secure, from American Express: www.creditsecure.com
- SmartCredit: www.smartcredit.com

Credit Scoring

- FICO
  901 Marquette Avenue
  Suite 3200
  Minneapolis, MN 55402
  (888) 342-6336
  www.myfico.com
  You can use this web site to get your credit score, learn about the history of credit scoring, and also see how your scores affect the rates you pay.
- Credit Karma
  www.creditkarma.com
  Offers free TransUnion scores, and lots of general information about credit scoring, including calculators and a score simulator.
- Credit Report ABC
  www.creditreportabc.com
  This service will help you challenge derogatory items on your credit report and get them removed, boosting your credit score. Also provides a lot of education about ways to boost your credit score.
- *Your Credit Score,* by Liz Pulliam Weston (FT Press, 2009). Updated, revised, smart guide that explains all you need to know about credit scoring.
- *The Complete Idiot's Guide to Improving Your Credit Score,* by Lita Epstein (Alpha Books, 2007). A decent summary about ways to improve your credit score.

ID Theft

- *Stopping Identity Theft,* by Scott Mitric (Nolo, 2009). A great overview by the CEO of an ID protection company.

- *Stolen Lives: Identity Theft Prevention Made Simple,* by John D. Sileo (DaVinci Publishing, 2005). My favorite book on this subject. Find even more info on Sileo's excellent web site, Think Like a Spy, at www.thinklikeaspy.com.
- Opt out: Stop prescreened credit offers by calling (888) 5OPTOUT (1-888-567-8688) or by registering at www.optout prescreen.com.
- Do Not Call: Stop annoying telemarketing by putting your name on the national Do Not Call Registry at www.donotcall .gov.
- Reduce junk mail: Cut down on junk mail by registering at the web site of the Direct Marketing Association (www.dmacon sumers.org).

Identity Protection Companies

- Lifelock
  www.lifelock.com/moneyanswers
  (800) 543-3562
  (mention promo code Moneyanswers to qualify for a discount)
- Identity Guard
  www.identityguard.com
  (800) 452-2541
- TrustedID
  www.trustedid.com
  (888) 548-7878

Mortgages

- HSH Associates
  237 West Parkway
  Pompton Plains, NJ 07444
  www.hsh.com
  (800) 873-2837
      This established and respected mortgage research firm hosts a web site replete with information about products, rates, and how to get the best deal on a home loan.
- Time Value Software
  www.timevalue.com/calculators/mortgage-comparison-calcu lator.aspx

This site hosts one of the best mortgage calculators on the Web.

- Closing.com
  www.closing.com
  Comparison shopping for the various services that are all built into the closing costs you pay when you get a new loan.

- ArcLoan
  www.arcloan.com
  (800) 272-5626
  Home of the mortgage in which the rate can only go down, not up.

- Mortgage Harmony
  www.mortgageharmony.com
  (800) 999-3764
  Watch this space for a brand-new mortgage product that is constantly ratcheting down rates, and never going up.

- Mortgage Modification
  www.modifymymortgage.com
  (800) 663-4396
  This company helps you make the best possible case to a mortgage lender about why you should qualify for a modification of your mortgage's interest rate and/or principal repayment terms in light of your financial circumstances. If appropriate, they can also help arrange a short sale of your home.

Reverse Mortgages

- AARP
  www.aarp.org/money/personal/reverse_mortgages/
  A comprehensive and consumerist site with lots of information about the pros and cons of reverse mortgages. Up-to-date with current rules and fees.

- National Center for Home Equity Conversion
  www.reverse.org
  This organization went inactive when its founder, Ken Scholen, moved over to AARP, but it has a lot of interesting information on its web site about the history of reverse mortgages.

- National Reverse Mortgage Lenders Association
  www.reversemortgage.org
    An informative site hosted by the industry trade group.

Shared Equity Mortgages

These three companies are currently offering shared equity (or shared appreciation) agreements.

- Rex & Company: www.rexagreement.com
- Equity Key: www.equitykey.com
- Grander Financial: www.granderfinancial.com

Equity Acceleration

These companies offer advice and products dealing with equity acceleration.

- Truth in Equity
  436 Leafy Way Avenue
  Spring Hill, FL 34606
  www.truthinequity.com
  (888) 262-5540
- Money Merge Account
  United First Financial
  Bluffdale, UT 84065
  (347) 445-0614
  www.unitedfirstfinancial.com/moneymergepage.html
- No More Mortgage
  444 West 600 South
  Lindon, UT 84042
  www.nomoremortgage.com
  (800) 598-1657
- Speed Equity
  www.speedequity.com
  (206) 414-2739
- *Own Your Home Years Sooner,* by Harj Gill (American Mortgage Eliminators Publishing, 2003).

Car Buying and Financing

- Zipcar
  www.zipcar.com
    An auto-sharing service that can be cheaper than a car rental.
- Hybrid tax breaks
  www.fueleconomy.gov
    Use this web site to find out which hybrids you can get tax breaks for buying.
- Hybrid calculator
  www.hybridcars.com/calculator/
    Are you better off keeping your clunker or buying a hybrid? Check this calculator to find out.
- TrueCar
  www.truecar.com
    This new site offers current real data showing what people in your area are actually paying for their cars. It amasses data from dealers and tax and licensing authorities. It also has good data on what the dealers themselves are paying.
- Edmunds
  www.edmunds.com
    The established leader in car consumer information, this site uses dealer data to calculate what it calls "true market value" pricing.
- CarQ
  www.carq.com
  (800) 517-2277
    My favorite car buying service. Even if you don't hire it, you'll learn a lot by visiting this site.
- Zag
  www.zag.com
    This web site aggregates several car buying services and discount deals so you can compare them before you choose how you want to buy your car.
- Capital One
  www.capitaloneautofinance.com
    This bank has committed a fair amount of money to being competitive on car loans.

Auto Leasing Calculators

Here are a few of my favorite spots on the Web for comparing lease and buy deals and learning more about leasing.

- www.leaseguide.com/leasevsbuy.htm
- www.dinkytown.net/java/BuyvsLease.html
- www.edmunds.com/calculators/auto_lease_calculator_index .html
- www.wheelsdirect2u.com

Education

- Saving for College: www.savingforcollege.com
  A clearinghouse of information about all aspects of saving for higher education.
- College Savings Plans Network: www.collegesavings.org
  A site sponsored by the states offering college plans.
- Morningstar: www.morningstar.com
  This research firm analyzes the best and worst 529 plans every year.
- FinAid: www.finaid.org
  The most authoritative web site about all matters pertaining to financial aid.
- FastWeb: www.fastweb.com
  The best place to hunt for college scholarships.
- Free Application for Federal Student Aid: www.fafsa.ed.gov
  This is the place where you'll find the correct forms for applying for federal financial aid, as well as guidance and directions.
- College Board: www.collegeboard.org
  This is a good source of information about student finance, as well as the site where you'll find forms for filing for private school–based financial aid.
- Project on Student Debt: www.ibrinfo.org
  An informative site for finding information about new income-based repayment plans for student loans.
- Simple Tuition: www.simpletuition.com
  A comparison-shopping site for student loans.

Peer Lending

- *The Complete Idiot's Guide to Person-to-Person Lending,* by Curtis E. Arnold and Beverly Blair Harzog (Alpha Books, 2009). A good overview of this area by a very smart guy.

These are the leading peer-to-peer lending sites:

- Virgin Money: www.virginmoneyus.com
- Prosper: www.prosper.com
- Fynanz, which specializes in student lending: www.fynanz.com
- Lending Club: www.lendingclub.com
- Loanio: www.loanio.com
- GreenNote: www.greennote.com

Credit Counseling

- Cambridge Credit Counseling
  www.cambridgecredit.org
  (800) 897-2200
    My favorite nonprofit debt counseling agency.
- U.S. Trustee, Department of Justice
  www.usdoj.gov/ust/eo/bapcpa/ccde/cc_approved.htm
    The federal government's list of approved credit counselors.
- National Foundation for Credit Counseling
  www.nfcc.org
  (800) 388-2227
    The first, most widely known, and most widely used non-profit credit counseling network.
- Association of Independent Consumer Credit Counseling Agencies
  www.aiccca.org
  (866) 703-8787
    A trade group of credit counseling firms, some for-profit and some nonprofit.
- American Association of Debt Management Organizations
  www.aadmo.org
  (281) 361-2325

A broad-based trade group, including credit counseling agencies and debt management firms.

Foreclosure

- Making Home Affordable
  www.makinghomeaffordable.gov
  (888) 995-HOPE
  The starting point for anyone with questions about the new government programs designed to help troubled homeowners.
- Fannie Mae
  www.fanniemae.com
  (800) 7FANNIE
- Freddie Mac
  www.freddiemac.com
  (800) FREDDIE
- Homeownership Preservation Foundation
  www.995hope.org
  This is a nonprofit public/private partnership designed to help troubled homeowners.
- Homeowner Crisis Resource Center
  www.housinghelpnow.org
  Sponsored by the National Foundation for Credit Counseling, this is a good place for troubled homeowners to get help.
- Housing and Urban Development Foreclosure Avoidance
  www.hud.gov/offices/hsg/sfh/hcc/hcs.cfm
  This site lists HUD-approved housing counseling agencies.
- *The Foreclosure Survival Guide,* by Stephen Elias (Nolo, 2008). A reassuring and smart guide by a consummate expert.
- *More Mortgage Meltdown,* by Whitney Tilson and Glenn Tongue (John Wiley & Sons, 2009). How to deal with mortgage problems.

Health Insurance, Expenses, and Debts

- eHealthInsurance
  www.ehealthinsurance.com

A good spot for comparison shopping health insurance plans if you must buy one for yourself.

- National Association of Insurance Commissioners
  www.naic.org
  This site, run by the regulators from all of the states, offers a comprehensive map of all the state-run risk pools for people who can't get affordable health insurance on their own.
- Medical Repricing
  www.medicalrepricing.com
  (877) 642-5657
  An alternative to traditional health insurance that gives you substantial discounts on everyday medical services and products, a limited medical benefit up to $10,000, and a high-deductible plan to cover major expenses over $10,000, for a far lower membership fee than traditional health insurance premiums would be. You can also get medical repricing even if you have a preexisting medical condition that would make it impossible to qualify for regular health insurance.
- HealthCare Advocates
  1420 Walnut Street, 9th Floor
  Philadelphia, PA 19102
  www.healthcareadvocates.com
  (215) 735-7711
  This company will help you find good, affordable doctors and negotiate medical bills down before you've incurred them, or after you are saddled with them.
- Patient Advocate Foundation
  700 Thimble Shoals Boulevard
  Suite 200
  Newport News, VA 23606
  www.patientadvocate.org
  (800) 532-5274
  There's a state-by-state guide to financial resources for medical care on the web site of this nonprofit advocacy organization.

Debt Collectors

- *Stop Debt Collectors: How to Protect Your Rights and Resolve Your Debts*, by Gerri Detweiler, Mary Reed, and John Ventura

(Credit.com, 2008). A good overview of your legal rights and how to make sure you use them correctly.
- Stop Collection Harassment: www.stopcollectionharassment .com

   A web site established by consumer lawyer Robert Stempler, with sample letters for consumers who want to do battle with their creditors and bill collectors.

Bankruptcy

- *The Bankruptcy Handbook*, by John Ventura (Kaplan Publishing, 2008). A comprehensive guide by a seasoned bankruptcy attorney.
- *The New Bankruptcy: Will It Work for You?*, by Stephen R. Elias (Nolo, 2009). An updated, detailed, yet simple guide by a consummate expert.
- Legal Consumer
   www.legalconsumer.com

   This is a comprehensive and very authoritative web site offering guidance to any consumer considering bankruptcy or going through it. It is hosted by experienced lawyers.
- American Bankruptcy Institute
   http://probono.abiworld.org/

   There's an interactive map on the web site of this professional association listing attorneys and legal clinics offering free advice and filing assistance to consumers considering bankruptcy.
- Rocket Lawyer Bankruptcy Center
   www.rocketlawyer.com/bankruptcy

   Another self-help legal site offering free forms and letters consumers can use in filing for bankruptcy protection.

About the Author

Jordan Elliot Goodman, frequently known as America's Money Answers Man, has been helping Americans improve their personal finances since he graduated from Columbia University's Graduate School of Journalism in 1977. He spent 18 years on the editorial staff at *Money* magazine, rising to become the magazine's Wall Street correspondent. He was a weekly financial commentator on *NBC News at Sunrise* for nine years and on Public Radio's *Marketplace Morning Report* for six years, and did a daily financial report on the Mutual Broadcasting System's *America in the Morning* show for eight years. He is the author of several best-selling books, including *Everyone's Money Book, The Dictionary of Finance and Investment Terms, Barron's Finance and Investment Handbook, Fast Profits in Hard Times,* and *Master Your Money Type.*

Mr. Goodman provides financial advice to millions of people each month through regular appearances on radio call-in shows on such stations as WLW in Cincinnati, KMOX in St. Louis, WHYN in Springfield (Massachusetts), WFLA in Tampa, and many more. He is a regular commentator on financial topics on national TV networks, including Fox, CNN, CNBC, and CBS, and many local and regional TV stations across the country, and gives frequent seminars to corporate, association, and university audiences. He hosts the popular personal finance web site at www.moneyanswers.com, and is the host of the weekly *Money Answers Show* on the VoiceAmerica Business Channel radio network (www.voiceamerica.com).

You can find out more about this book at www.masteryourdebt.com.

Index